WONDER WHERE ALL THE WONDER WENT?

CLUES TO FINDING WONDER IN THIS WORLD

Ronald Higdon

Energion Publications
Gonzalez, FL
2021

Copyright © 2021, Ronald Higdon

Unless otherwise notated, Scripture quotations are taken from the New Revised Standard Version, copyright 1989 by the Division of Christian Education & National Council of the Churches of Christ.

Scripture quotations marked TNIV are taken from Today's New International Version, copyright 2001, 2005 by International Bible Society. Used by permission of International Bible Society. All rights reserved worldwide.

Scripture quotations marked NLT are taken from the Holy Bible, New Living Translation, copyright 1996, 2004, 2007, 20013 by Tyndale House Foundation. Used by permission of Tyndale House Publishers, Inc. Carol Stream, Illinois 60188. All rights reserved.

Scripture quotations marked NJB are taken from the New Jerusalem Bible, copyright 1985 by Darton, Longman, & Todd, Ltd. & Doubleday.

Scripture quotations marked NKJV are taken from The Holy Bible, *New King James Version,* copyright 1979, 1980, 1982 by Thomas Nelson, Inc. Nashville, Tennessee.

Cover Image: Adobe Stock # 202797365

ISBN: 978-1-63199-751-8
eISBN: 978-1-63199-752-5

Library of Congress Control Number: 2021940029

Energion Publications
P.O. Box 841
Gonzalez, FL 32560

850-525-3916

Energion.com
pub@energion.com

Dedication

This book is dedicated to the countless individuals
who have kept wonder alive in my world
and taught me how to find it
even in the most difficult times.

Table of Contents

Prologue	Childhood Wonder	vii
1	Cultivate a mind-set for wonder	1
2	Be On the Listen	11
3	Be On the Lookout	19
4	Be Quick to Offer Praise and Thanksgiving	27
5	Read, Read, Read — Write, Write, Write	35
6	Stay off the Defensive and the Critical	45
7	Get Into Trouble the Way Jesus Did	53
8	Determine to Make a Difference In Your World	61
9	Refuse To Live On Automatic	69
10	Make Yourself a Humor Being	77
11	Commit to Downward Mobility	85
12	Keep Using Your Kingdom Glasses	93
Epilogue	Wonder in God's Broken World	101
	Bibliography of Quoted Sources	103

Prologue

Childhood Wonder

> Turn back, turn back, O time in your flight
> Make me a child again — just for tonight.
> — Elizabeth Akers Allen

As the years pass, memories often leap to a new level; they become literally larger than life. Gratefully, some were larger than life to begin with. My mother never tired of relating my first trip as a child of six to Louisville's old-fashioned amusement park, *Fontaine Ferry* (commonly called *Fountain Ferry*). In comparison to the mega-parks of today it was relatively small; all walking surfaces were sawdust covered (more like small wooden shavings), providing a unique kind of feeling as one entered the gates.

My six-year-old response (according to all adult family members present) was one of unbridled ecstasy: I simply couldn't stop jumping up and down with joyous exclamations. It was a wonder to behold and, evidently, so was I. Leave it to a six-year-old to express unbridled delight to the delight of the smiling adults who witnessed his demonstration. It's in my memory bank only because of those who later told me about it. My only question has been: wonder where all that wonder went?

The other childhood parallel, which I do remember, was my first experience at a "three-ring-circus." Under a huge tent, three rings of eye-popping acrobatics and other acts were performed to the accompaniment of a circus band. I have an old record of some of the music those bands provided for various acts; it is easy to visualize the performers as you listen to music found only at the circus. Putting aside for the moment the possible mistreatment of animals in some of the acts (this is beyond the dimensions of our subject), there was nothing like what went on under that tent in a TV-less world that was not plagued by endless entertainment. You can catch the flavor of what it was like in the 1952 Cecil B. DeMille movie *The Greatest Show on Earth*. The spectacular circus parade that was part of the show was indeed a wonder to behold.

Beyond Childhood Wonder

Our remembered childhoods are filled with one wonder after another, primarily because everything was new to us. Everything was fresh and alive. Everything was a "first." No wonder they were wonders! As we age and everything echoes with the famous "been there, done that," does this mean that wonder is to be found no more? *Toyland* sings about the wonders of the world of play and imagination that, once you leave, you can never return again. But are there not wonders for every age in our journey through life? Are there not wonders of different kinds and different dimensions that should cause just as much jumping for joy as a six-year-old at his first amusement park? Are there not always wonders to behold and amaze for those who have eyes to see, ears to hear, and a lifestyle (faith-style) that prepares one to be aware of them?

That's what this book is about. It's about recapturing (or finding for the first time) some of the joys of existence — even in the midst of a COVID-19 pandemic. It's about learning to sing the Lord's song in a strange land and a strange time. It's about finding the spark that brings your first thought on arising each morning:

This is the day the Lord has made; I will rejoice and be glad in it (Psalm 118:24).

Although in one sense, wonder is always a gift, in another sense, it is an achievement. It is an achievement in response to Jesus' command to all of his disciples in every age, "*Therefore, keep awake*" (Mark 13:35). This book is an attempt to respond to that wake-up call.

Here are some of the steps we'll take in our journey:

1. Cultivating and maintaining a mindset for wonder is possible and this book attempts to give some pointers on how to do it.
2. The place to begin is to discipline ourselves to become better listeners in every situation.
3. Being present, focused and looking with eyes that see, is a necessary, developed skill.
4. Praise and thanksgiving give the extra gifts of making us aware of so much more for which to be grateful.
5. In a Facebook and blog culture, it is mandatory that we read that which inspires and enlarges our lives. (Many suggestions are offered in this chapter.) Don't forget the frequently surprising benefits of writing.
6. A negative attitude of criticism and defensiveness will literally close your eyes and your ears to the wonders that are right before you.
7. If you get into trouble for the reasons Jesus did, you will find yourself living in a much larger grace-filled world.
8. Know that you can make a difference in your corner of the world — regardless of its size or location.
9. Live a life of self-reflection and awareness that enables you to make more appropriate and helpful responses.
10. Recognize the healing and liberating power of a sense of humor that makes it possible not to take yourself too seriously.
11. Learn the wisdom and the life-opening possibilities of Jesus' great paradox: "The first shall be last and the last shall be first."

12. Put on your Kingdom glasses and don't take them off. Without them you'll never see things as they really are.

Each chapter is divided into the following sections: Setting the Stage; Reflections; Excursus; Summation; Questions for Reflection and Conversation. The Bibliography includes every book quoted; the listing does not imply agreement with everything written in each book.

Cultivate a Mind-Set for Wonder

SETTING THE STAGE

> *This is the day the Lord has made.*
> *We will rejoice and be glad in it.*
> Psalm 118:24 (NLT).

The "original blessing" of creation (created in the image and likeness of God) gave every human being an inherent dignity, which I am calling in this book your True Self and your immortal diamond.[1]

Richard Rohr's designation of the Genesis account of creation being about something other than "original sin" is quite refreshing. The end of each day's creation is pronounced "good" and at the end of the sixth "day" God does two things not done on any of the other "days." First: Genesis 1:28 tells us that *God blessed* those whom he had made in his image. Second: God takes a panoramic survey of all he has made: *and he saw that it was excellent in every way* (NLT). The NRSV uses the traditional *very good* translation

---

1 Richard Rohr, *Immortal Diamond* (San Francisco: Jossey-Bass, 2013), 121.

but for me *excellent* carries the full impact of how God judges his creation.

Many have noted that the Bible never uses the term "original sin." This concept comes from the 5th century Augustine. As some of my more conservative friends would say, "It is not a part of the original autographs." To speak of "original blessing" does not mean that something didn't go wrong in the garden, but that the biggest word to be remembered from God's initial activity is blessing. That certainly seems to be what the message and ministry of Jesus was all about. Grace, mercy, love, possibility, and opportunity are the big words that appear to upset those who demanded that life be lived by the letter of the Law (613 of them to be exact) and that every transgression was to be duly noted and punished accordingly. Jesus kept reminding the legalists that they missed the bigger and more important things of life and faith. After reading Genesis 1 and 2, it might be a good practice to then read the Gospels in this order: Mark (the first one written), Matthew, Luke, and John. It will make you a believer in "original blessing."

REFLECTIONS

Waiting

Samuel Beckett's 1952 production of *Waiting for Godot* was voted the most significant English language play of the twentieth century. Two characters sit on an empty stage engaging in conversation and encounters while waiting for someone named Godot, who never shows up. Beckett warned his critics not to read too much into the play, but that hasn't stopped an avalanche of interpretations.

Whoever (or whatever) they are waiting for never comes. It's just a waiting game. Does it speak to those of us who often find ourselves waiting for the right person or the right time or the right opportunity in order to get on with life? How often have we heard ourselves saying, "When I.........then things will really be different and I'll be ready."

"In the meantime" is a phrase I think was made famous in countless western movies when the narrator said, "Meanwhile back at the ranch," which indicated a shift in the action of the film. Life goes on, and is meant to go on, in the meantime of whatever it is we are waiting for. What we are waiting for may never come but "in the meantime" always comes. It is the time and place that calls for investment and a mindset for wonder.

Back to normal

A repeated phrase in today's world of restrictions and limitations imposed by the COVID-19 pandemic is: "when things get back to normal." Never mind that the word *normal* is usually not defined but when it does begin to be unpacked, we discover a multitude of ideas about what "normal" ought to look like. Those of us who are enduring months of "quarantine fatigue" are certain of at least one thing normal should contain. That is why we keep singing "Don't fence me in," knowing all the while that's where we really want to be until this pandemic cools down, vaccines become available, and it is once again safe to mix and mingle.

Maintaining a mindset for wonder during these days is no easy task. When I talk about wonder, I'm talking, among other things, about something that takes you out of yourself, that brings a sense of awe, that lifts you into another dimension of time (or even makes time seem to stand still), that almost brings an electrifying sensation, that brings the assurance of being loved and accepted in a universe full of God's grace. If you are a reader of history, you soon discover that wonder has never been reserved for normalcy but has especially been available during some of the darkest and most difficult days in the past. Victor Frankl discovered wonder in the hell of a Nazi concentration camp, although it is more accurate to say that the wonder was actually in him and not in the camp. It was his mindset and he brought it with him.

Developing that mindset

A theme that will be repeated in various ways in this book is the reminder that any real secret of life is within us. Security is not out there, it is within. Peace is not out there, it is within. Self-esteem is not out there, it is within. Confidence is not out there, it is within. Courage is not out there, it is within. And the list goes on. In one sense, I bring to life all that I really want out of life. It is my mindset, my perspective, my philosophy, my purpose, my goals, my sense of calling, and my commitment to a special set of values that determine the direction my life will take. I take great care in nurturing that which is within me.

Those nagging (and debilitating) murmurings like envy, jealousy, and resentment are wonder-destroyers of the first order. They both blind and deafen us to the wonders that wait to be seen and heard in our present world — just where we are and as we are. That is why Scripture, devotional reading, and self-reflective prayer are always a must at the beginning of each day. When people ask how they should pray, I suggest that a good way to begin each day is by imagining that the Lord asks us, "Tell me what is bothering you about this day. What are you going to have to deal with that troubles you most? Who are you going to have to meet that challenges your relational skills? Why do you think this so?" The more concrete and honest our praying is, the more likely we are to be ready with a wonder mindset for the day.

> My personal sidebar: A famous newspaper motto is: "All the news that's fit to print." Today it appears to mean all the news that gives us a fit (although we must provide our own fit).

I have found it necessary to cut back on media time (newscasts) in order to avoid becoming a cynic about national politics and a pessimist about the state of the nation and the world at large. Each newscast may end with a bright spot but this two or three-minute segment does not make up for the countless previous segments of incivility, mayhem, and chaos. (I read somewhere that it takes five positive statements to offset one negative utterance.

Does that mean we ought to hear and see more positive things than we do negative things? In a word, yes!) As a "primary" in Sunday School (a term no longer used), I remember a song that has these lines: "Be careful little eyes what you see; be careful little ears what you hear." This is not the call to be ill-informed or ignorant of what is transpiring in our world; it is the challenge to avoid negative saturation and overkill.

As you are careful about what you eat, be just as careful with what you feed your mind. Every day give yourself mega-doses of courage, faith (trust), hope, love, mercy, and a sense of being God's person in God's world for such a time as this. Ten minutes a day won't do it! Sometimes we seniors find shaking heads at our love for "feel good" movies. My question: "Feel bad movies are better?" I'll try to hold myself to just a few rants: I do enjoy movies like *Places in the Heart* and *Fried Green Tomatoes* and I do not enjoy movies with a script that can't find anything better than an "F" word every other line and supplies violence (and blood) at levels never seen before. Perhaps I continue to be influenced by the song I heard as a primary. I certainly hope so.

EXCURSUS

> Cynicism may seem a mild transgression, but it is a patient predator that suffocates hope, slowly, over the years, like the honey mushroom which forces itself between the bark and sapwood of a tree and over decades is strangled to death.[2]

> I can't begin to heal until I've acknowledged my pain, and I can't acknowledge my pain until I've kicked my dependence on cynicism. Cynicism is a powerful anesthetic, we use it to numb ourselves to pain, but which also, by its nature, numbs us to truth and joy. Grief is healthy. Even anger can be healthy.

---

2   Rachel Held Evans, *Searching for Sunday* (Nashville: Nelson Books, 2015), 87.

But numbing ourselves with cynicism in an effort to avoid feeling those things is not.[3]

When life continues to disappoint, it is so much easier to become a cynic than to do anything about those things we are allowing to cause our unhappiness. Cynicism is one way to shut ourselves off from the red flags that are calls for attention and action. Anything that shuts us off from life is what I term a life-subtractor; by their very nature they are not able to add anything to life. And all we bring to life should be additions and not subtractions.

There's hardly anything in life that ever lives up to our full expectations. We usually enter new projects or new relationships with the best-case scenarios in place and are left unprepared for the inevitable setbacks and disappointments that begin to surface. I recently read that most new businesses fail because the planners were only expecting the best possible results from their efforts and didn't include "repair kits" in their on-going management equipment. The motto, "Expect the best but plan for the worst," sounds pessimistic but it captures the inevitable paradoxes that come with every endeavor. Perfection is simply not the order of the day.

As we get older, a temptation is to bemoan the loss of the "good old days" (which never were as good as our selective memoires now recall them) and become experts as volunteer private eyes for the detection of flaws, imperfections, and just plain wrong. (A brief historical survey reveals these have always been present in abundance). It is true in life as it is in biblical study: You find what you are looking for. Also, chronic complainers and habitual nay-sayers are usually not the ones who make positive contributions.

The inscription on the General Motors Building at the World's Fair of 1933 read: "The world will never starve for wonders, but only for want of wonder." A sense of wonder lifts the human spirit to another dimension and may be one of the reasons Jesus said that unless we become like little children, we will not be able to enter the

---

3   Ibid, 222.

Kingdom of God (Mark 10:15). I think N. T. Wright summarizes our basis for wonder:

> The first Christians, being first-century Jews who believed that Israel's God had fulfilled his ancient promises in Jesus of Nazareth, were what I call "creational monotheists": that is, they believed that the one creator God, having made the world, remained in active and dynamic relation with it.[4]

If we continue in the line of "creational monotheists," we become those who live in a world of wonder. We look for it and find it; we listen for it and hear it. (More about these in the next two chapters). Webster's New World College Dictionary defines wonder this way: "a person, thing, or event that causes astonishment and admiration: marvel. Feeling of surprise, admiration. To be seized with wonder. Have curiosity, sometimes mingled with doubt." Biblically, we would expand that definition (keeping the doubt!) and add: "wonders in another dimension."

Victor Frankl's classic *Man's Search for Meaning* provides a graphic journey through "life" in a Nazi death-camp. "We who lived in the concentration camps can remember the men who walked through the huts comforting others, giving away their last piece of bread. They may have been few in number, but they offer sufficient proof that everything can be taken from a man but one thing: the last of the human freedoms — to choose one's attitude in any given set of circumstances, to choose one's own way."[5]

These are the kinds of wonders that touch, not only our hearts, but our souls. These are the wonders that come because someone has spoken or done that which lies beyond human explanation. It is for lack of this kind of wonder that the world will surely die. (Remember the 1933 World's Fair posting?)

---

4   N. T. Wright, *The Case for the Psalms* (New York: HarperOne, 2013), 17.
5   Victor Frankl, *Man's Search for Meaning* (Boston: Beacon Press, 1959), 65.

SUMMATION

> ...in no time the four of us were remarking on the social and economic and political aspects of that phenomenon — lest an assertively unqualified psychology be allowed to strip a particular human scene of its thickly textured complexity.[6]

The demand to cultivate a mindset for wonder always comes in the context of "thickly textured complexity." That is why the task is always so challenging. If you are waiting for simpler times or less demanding situations, you are doomed to wait in vain. As I write these words, we are in the midst of the COVID-19 pandemic, demonstrations for changes in police policies, outbursts of looting and burning in some of our major cities, and the usual divisions in our political world with insults and labels flying. None of these issues can be addressed with simple slogans like, "Let's just all get along." Each one is loaded with "thickly textured complexity" and calls for much more than bumper-sticker simplicity.

A Texas story tells of a rancher who bought ten ranches and put them together to form one giant spread. A friend asked the name of his new mega-ranch. "It's called the Circle Q, Rambling Brook, Double Bar, Broken Circle, Crooked Creek, Golden Horseshoe, Lazy B, Bent Arrow, Triple O Ranch." "Wow," exclaimed his friend, "I bet you have a lot of cattle." "Not really," lamented the rancher. "Not many survive the branding."[7]

Statistics do not permit me to say "not many," but observations have led me to conclude that "far too many" do not survive the brandings life places on them: disappointments, setbacks, illnesses, tragedies, as well as the general unfairness and inequities that permeate all human existence. Those who don't survive the brandings don't necessarily stop breathing; they succumb to the deadly dis-eases of anger, bitterness and resentment that quickly drain away life-giving qualities — like wonder. In the chapters

---

6   Robert Coles, *Harvard Diary II* (New York: Crossroad Publishing, 1997), 51.
7   *Homiletics*, Volume 10, Number 2, March-April, 1998, 66.

that follow I will try to describe some of things we can do that will help us develop a mindset for wonder in spite of some brandings that will not fade away.

A final question: What wonders have I missed because I didn't expect to find any?

QUESTIONS FOR REFLECTION AND DISCUSSION

1. How do you begin your day? Do you see it in line with Psalm 118:24?
2. What are the things you find most detrimental to developing a mindset for wonder?
3. In this opening chapter, what spoke most directly or clearly to you? Why do you think this was so?

BE ON THE LISTEN

SETTING THE STAGE

>*Again he began to teach beside the sea….He began to teach them many things in parables, and in his teaching he said to them: "Listen!"* (Mark 4:1-2).
>
>*"Let anyone with ears listen!"* (Matthew 13:9).
>
>*Then his disciples asked him what this parable meant…."Now the parable is this: The seed is the word of God…as for that in the good soil, these are the ones who, when they hear the word, hold it fast in an honest and good heart, and bear fruit with patient endurance."* (Luke 8:9, 11, 15).
>
>Listening is more of a mindset than a checklist of dos and don'ts.[8]

How did we miss this?

All three synoptic Gospels (Matthew, Mark, and Luke) relate Jesus' story that Matthew calls "The Parable of the Sower." The parables are almost identical in wording with the first word in Matthew and Mark being an exclamatory "Listen!" This can

---
8   Kate Murphy, *You're Not Listening*, 22.

easily be paraphrased: "Now hear this!" The more appropriate designation for what Jesus tells is: "A Parable About the Ways We Listen." Each of the three stories ends with the same command: "Let anyone with ears listen!" The very first designated "parable" in each of the first three Gospels is about listening and it is the only parable where Jesus explains its meaning in response to the disciples' request. (Sidebar: the KJV translation uses "hearken" in Mark and "behold" in Matthew.)

> In first-century Palestine, it is estimated that nearly 97 percent of the Jewish peasantry could neither read nor write, a not unexpected figure for predominantly oral societies such as the one in which Jesus lived.[9]

In an oral culture, how people listened was always of primary importance to any speaker. It is too quickly forgotten that those who first received the gospel didn't read it, they heard it. The four Gospels were read aloud and so were the letters of Paul (written before any of the Gospels). Many scholars have concluded that the readings were "enacted" presentations with animated facial expressions, motions, and, perhaps, even props. Reading to groups was an art form designed to make the listening easier and the hearing more accurate.

Exclamations at the beginning and the end

Jesus' parable is introduced with the single word "Listen!" and concludes with the same word: "Listen!" I cannot imagine a more dramatic way to underscore what needed to be said with more force; a simple, "This is very important," would hardly have been sufficient. Its location as the first parable in each of the Gospels, its call to attention word at the beginning and the end, the fact that it is the only parable Jesus fully explains to his disciples, makes it unique. The immediate attention-grabbing device, calling to mind the opening word of the Jewish Shema, did not go unnoticed by

---

9   Reza Aslan, *Zealot* (New York: Random House, 2013), 34.

the crowd: *"Hear, O Israel: The Lord is our God, the Lord alone. You shall love the Lord your God with all your heart, and with all your soul, and with all your might* (Deuteronomy 6:4). The Shema was recited morning and evening as part of Jewish daily prayers. Some translate the opening words: *"Listen, O Israel...."* The Greek word translated "Listen!" in our translation of the parable can just as easily be translated "Hear!" but I believe that "Listen!" better captures the intention of the parable.

REFLECTIONS

> "I'm a better listener than most people," said a trial lawyer in Houston returning my call in his car during rush-hour traffic. "Wait, hold on a second, I have another call."[10]

I think the trial lawyer is just about on par with most of what passes for listening in our culture today. My question: knowing the call he was returning had to do with research about how we listen, why did he return it in his car during rush-hour traffic? The challenge of driving under those conditions should have taken his full attention. Another question: How many things in this present culture ever get our full attention? (Even as I write these lines, I am finishing a bowl of cereal for breakfast! So, there I am: Guilty as charged!) There seems to be some built-in sense that if we are not doing at least two things at once we are wasting time.

In a book on time-management, I remember finding a chapter on our need to separate the urgent from the important. When the distinction fails to be made, we find ourselves like the lawyer, interrupting an important conversation to respond to the ringing of a call that *might* be something we don't want to miss. Following through on the important is a much better strategy than trying to grab everything that happens to fly by calling for our attention. If we are not careful, we end up not giving our full attention to anything.

---

10 Kate Murphy, *You're Not Listening, 19.*

> Good listeners are not born that way, they become that way.[11]

We can train/discipline ourselves to become better listeners. It is an acquired skill. It is an intentional decision. Its first basic rule is one that always gets a unanimous vote but not unanimous practice:

> It will be fair to say that "presence" is the cornerstone of all true spirituality, regardless of ethnic or cultural origin.... The Gospels are filled with statements of Jesus that begin with words like *"Beware"* (be aware), *"Look," "Hear and understand."*[12]

I remember contests being advertised with this spelled out in bold type: YOU MUST BE PRESENT TO WIN. That can be written across almost all of the significant things in life: like spirituality, like listening. Most of us recognize when someone is powerfully "present." Dr. Wayne Oates was one of the most "present" persons I have ever known. The father of pastoral counseling and the author of over fifty books, you never felt you were competing for his attention when he spoke to you and listened to you. He was never glancing around the room to see if there was someone else he wanted to speak to. He talked with you until the conversation was completed. As one fortunate enough to have several sessions with him, I can testify that just being in his presence for 50 minutes was therapeutic.

> "So, this was your first flight. Were you scared?" "Well, to tell the truth, I didn't dare put my full weight down on the seat."[13]

I don't know if there is a parallel between being half-seated and half-present but I think such an uncomfortable position is evident in both situations. In being fully present, it is necessary

---

11 Ibid, 69.
12 Kenneth S. Long, *The Zen Teachings of Jesus* (New York: Crossroad, 2001), 44.
13 Niles Eliot Goldstein, *God at the Edge* (New York: Bell Tower, 2000), 25.

to let your full weight down so that you can bring your physical and emotional being into play. According to studies, because we are able to process what is being said faster than the person we are listening to is able to speak, there is sufficient space for wandering thoughts if we don't concentrate on remaining focused.

EXCURSUS

> It brings to mind an often-told story about the late Dick Bass, son of a Texas oil baron. He was known for going on ambitious mountain-climbing expeditions and talking about them, at length, to anyone within earshot, including a man who happened to be seated next to him on an airplane. For the duration of the cross-country flight, Bass went on about the treacherous peaks of McKinley and Everest and about the time he almost died in the Himalayas and his plan to climb Everest again. As they were about to land, Bass realized he hadn't properly introduced himself. "That's okay," the man said, extending his hand. "I'm Neil Armstrong. Nice to meet you."[14]

Those of us who are "talkers" are brought up short by this account and Kate Murphy's commentary: "You miss out on opportunities (and you can look like an idiot) when you don't take a breath and listen. Talking about yourself doesn't add anything to your knowledge base. Again, you already know about you."[15] It makes me wonder how much I have missed and how many times my clever monologue made me look like an idiot. When I compare my "small steps" with the "giant leap" Neil Armstrong made stepping onto the face of the moon, I'm certain I have lost some giant opportunities to add to my knowledge base, not even considering the enriching experience of getting to know another human being. All I had to do was stop talking and listen. Really listen….and not just to those from whom I thought I might learn a lot.

---

14 Kate Murphy, *You're Not Listening*, 68.
15 Ibid, 68.

One renowned and highly educated Desert Father was found by his apprentices to be speaking at length with a local peasant. Later that evening he was asked by the younger brothers why he, such a learned man who even knew Sanskrit, was speaking to this illiterate worker. In response, he simply replied, "Ah yes, I do know many things. But I know not one word of 'peasant.'"[16]

This Desert Father did not fall into the trap Paul warns about in I Corinthians 8:1 — *Knowledge puffs up but love builds up*. What little I know about the Desert Fathers leads me to conclude that the one in the related incident did not believe his knowledge made him more important than the peasant. He must have believed that even an illiterate peasant needed to be heard on the level ground of a human being created in the image of God. This particular Desert Father knew how important it was to know the words of "peasant." His knowledge was incomplete without them. His work of love was lacking without their inclusion. His listening requirements needed to include this peasant in order to be complete. The peasant was no Neil Armstrong, but this was one whose feet had walked places the Desert Father had never been.

SUMMATION

Writing this brief chapter has brought more than a little regret. Too much of our time is spent in trying to sell ourselves or some idea we know people simply can't live without. Another place I recognized myself was in a New Yorker cartoon: a guy holding a glass of wine at a cocktail party says, "Behold, as I guide the conversation to my narrow area of expertise."[17] One subtle way of doing this I have heard on more than one occasion: "That reminds me of the time when I was...." Thus, is provided a change of focus, a change of direction, and a different person on center stage.

---

16 Robert J. Wicks, *Crossing the Desert* (Notre Dame: Sorin Books, 2007), 115.
17 Kate Murphy, *You're Not Listening*, 19.

Wonder Where the Wonder Went

It is no accident that Jesus' first designated parable is about the ways people listen. One of these ways simply provides deaf ears. One of these ways doesn't provide enough depth to provide a change to take root. One of these ways gets quickly choked out by other concerns or distractions. One of these ways is productive and provides benefits that seem to just keep growing. Being willing to see ourselves at one time or another as all four of these hearers can help us to discover ways to be more active in our listening. Listening is our way of connecting. It is really our way of remaining in relationship. I'm convinced it is really one of the major ways we stay alive.

A final question: what wonders have I missed simply because I wasn't listening?

QUESTIONS FOR REFLECTION AND CONVERSATION

1. Were you surprised by Jesus' strong emphasis on listening at the beginning of his ministry?
2. Have you thought about ways in which you might improve your listening skills?
3. What lessons do you feel we can learn by contrasting the Neil Armstrong and Desert Father stories?

3
BE ON THE LOOKOUT

SETTING THE STAGE

>(Jesus to his disciples): *"Do you have eyes, and fail to see? Do you have ears, and fail to hear?"* (Mark 8:18).

>Ludwig Wittgenstein: "Don't think. Look!"[18]

The full tragedy of not seeing is being unaware of our condition. Following the healing of the man born blind and his being thrown out of the synagogue, Jesus tells him: *"I came into this world for judgment so that those who do not see may see, and those who do see may become blind."* Some Pharisees who were standing nearby heard him and said, *"Surely we are not blind are we?"* (John 9:39-40). This complex exchange requires more than surface exegesis, but it clearly speaks to how easy it is to look and fail to grasp the meaning of what is seen.

We too easily dismiss the fact that Jesus healed the blind man on the Sabbath; this was no small matter for those whose who considered themselves the guardians of the Torah. Care on the

---

18 Kenneth Long, *The Zen Teachings of Jesus*, 181.

Sabbath was sanctioned, cure on the Sabbath was forbidden. In his post-healing discussion with the Pharisees, the healed man contended that no one who was a sinner (accused of being so because of his sabbath breaking) could do what Jesus did. All the man knew was: *"One thing I know, that though I was blind, now I see"* (John 9:25).

"The Pharisees evidently did too much thinking and not enough looking" (Wittgenstein — from a lost source). Shifting the emphasis to ourselves, the question becomes: Do we know how to be on the lookout and not permit our vision to be distorted by preconceived notions of what is expected and accepted in our fields of vision? As with listening, seeing requires discipline, education, and openness. If what we see is too disturbing, are we guilty of turning a blind-eye? Somewhere I read that when a verse of Scripture begins with *"Behold!"* it's like grabbing someone by the shirt collar to get their attention. "Behold" is the shift from "Now hear this," to "Now see this." It seems people have always needed attention grabbers to get them to see what is right in front of them.

REFLECTIONS

And the angel of the Lord appeared to him in a flaming fire from the midst of the bush, and he saw and behold! (Exodus 3:2, KJV).

When the Lord saw that he had turned aside to see, God called to him out of the bush, "Moses! Moses!" (Exodus 3:4).

Earth's crammed with heaven,
And every common bush afire with God.
But only he who sees takes off his shoes;
The rest sit round it and pluck blackberries.
 — Elizabeth Barret Browning

A frequent command from teachers is, "Now pay attention!" This classroom jargon would tell us that Moses decides to pay attention to the strange sight he glimpses out of the corner of his eye.

When God sees his focus, he calls Moses by name (Exodus 3:4). This text raises all sorts of interesting questions: Does God notice when we notice? Will God refrain from speaking until he has our undivided attention? There immediately comes to mind the advice of Eli to the young Samuel who hears his name being called and thinks the old man is asking for service of some kind. Eli perceives something profound is occurring and instructs Samuel to respond the next time he hears his name with, *"Speak Lord, for your servant is listening"* (I Samuel 3:9). In so doing, Samuel signals he is ready to hear and respond in obedience.

Biblically speaking, "casual listening" and "casual looking" don't seem to garner many significant results. The looking and the seeing in almost every instance develop into something that reaches beyond the mere physical. II Kings 6:17 illustrates this idea. Elisha's servant gets up one morning and sees the horses and chariots of the Aramean army surrounding them. He laments: *"Alas, master, what shall we do?"* Elisha responds with the much used preaching text: *"Do not be afraid, for there are more with us than there are with them.* Then: *Elisha prayed, "O Lord, please open his eyes that he may see." So the Lord opened the eyes of the servant, and he saw; the mountains were full of horses and chariots of fire all around Elisha* (II Kings 6:16-17). We might compare this seeing with the eyes of faith to listening with the ear of the heart. Full seeing and hearing involve another dimension of reality.

> To see a world in a grain of sand
> And a Heaven in a Wild flower,
> Hold infinity in the palm of your hand
> And eternity in an hour.
> — William Blake

We might summarize this first section with a general rule of thumb: There is always more to be seen than will ever be available to the casual observer.

EXCURSUS

> It seems those most likely to miss God's work in the world are those most convinced they know exactly what to look for, the ones who expect God to play by the rules.[19]
>
> As you strive to keep your focus on the present moment, you can experience the full wonder of "here."[20]

Every religious tradition has some statement about the importance of living in the present moment, of living in the now, of being focused on where you are and what is going on around you. You can't begin your day with a determination to look for wonder because that is almost a guarantee that you will spend your time looking in all the wrong places. It is in the "full wonder of here" that wonder is discovered. A post-modern movie-musical, *Moulin Rouge*, lures its customers with promises of "Spectacular! Spectacular!" That is a kind of "in your face wonder" that is dazzling and provocative but not very helpful in gendering the awe and spiritual wonder that reaches into the very heart and soul of existence. Often, real wonder displays a very ordinary face (Note: I also used this story in another book):

> A missionary working in Cambodia tells of taking a $200 gift from friends in the United States to throw a party for children from the barrios. He hired a bus to take them to a park, provided games to play, and all kinds of good food to eat. He exclaimed, "What a day it was!" Then he writes: "Some of the children hung around the bus for a few moments at the end of the day. I turned to a little smiling girl of eight and asked her what was the best thing she liked from the day. In response she looked up at me and said, 'When you took my hand as we walked back to the bus.'"[21]

---

19 Rachel Held Evans, *Searching for Sunday*, 90.
20 Cherie Carter-Scott, *If Life is a Game…These are the Rules* (Naperville, IL: Simple Truths, 1998), 85.
21 Robert J. Wicks, *Riding the Dragon* (Notre Dame: Sorin Books, 2012), 107-108.

I have always found it interesting that the longest stretch of time in the Liturgical Year is called "Ordinary Time." It is a time for growth and development and has none of the extraordinary events that mark Advent, Easter, or Pentecost. Most of our lives are lived in this ordinary kind of time.; day follows day with the routines of existence filling most of our time. Frederick Buechner offers this reminder: "If we really had our eyes open, we would see that all moments are key moments."[22] The Incarnation is the great reminder that all time is sacred time and all ground is holy ground. The greatest biblical miracle is the story of God's stepping on the world's stage in the form of a baby and casting his lot with us in all of our journeys through this very earthy existence.

The transformation of that earthy existence into something full of wonder, is what we are to be on the lookout for. It is not in abandoning life, but in embracing it fully that we discover the gifts of existence and the grace of God's goodness. This means we never overlook the unlikely. When Nathanael is informed by Philip that the one foretold by Moses and the prophets has been found in Nazareth, he has one question: *Can anything good come out of Nazareth?* (John 2:46). Nazareth was regarded as a nothing little place that didn't even merit a notation in Hebrew Scripture. Everybody knew the Messiah could not possibly come from such an unimportant place. Philip doesn't offer any argument, he simply issues the invitation, *"Come and see."* The way to make discoveries of wonder in the unexpected places is simply to be willing to take a look. Don't write off any place where God can work his wonders; don't write off any person through whom God can work the miracles of his grace; don't write off any unorthodox method God might adopt to accomplish his work.

> ...chaos theory, combined with quantum theory gives a one-two punch to the older deterministic model of a closed universe....The laws of physics still work, but in the context of a wide-open system that has been dubbed "chaotic." One

---

22 Frederick Buechner, *Listening to Your Life* (New York: HarperSanFrancisco, 1992), 50.

need no longer do logical gymnastics to make a case for the intervention of God into the old closed universe of Newton. Instead, chaos theory suggests that the universe is not closed at all, but wide open for God to interact with creation from the subatomic to the cosmic levels. Rather than thinking of the intervention of God and the suspension of the laws of nature, chaos theory suggests an open universe in which God has freedom of expression.[23]

While confessing my only partial understanding of chaos and quantum theories, I grasp enough to concur with Harry Lee Poe in his above comments. The discovery that the "systems" governing this universe are not characterized by "fixity" but by an amazing openness has transformed our understanding of God's relationship to our world and our lives. Phrases like, *Is anything too hard for the Lord?* and *All things are possible for God,* take on new meaning. In insisting that "God must play by the rules," many ruled out much of the miracle that is liberally sprinkled through the pages of the Bible. Now we understand that those "rules" are larger than we imagined and have much more flexibility built into them. It really does "suggest an open universe in which God has freedom of expression."

SUMMATION

Frederick Longbridge (1847-1922), British clergyman and author, is credited with writing: "Two men look through the same bars — one sees mud and one sees stars." Dale Carnegie supplied a more popular version: "Two men looked out from prison bars. One saw mud, the other saw stars." (From a lost source).

Many have asked about a piece of literature, "How do you read that?" Others have perceptually asked, "How do you see that?" What we read or what we see is much more complex than what is on the printed page or what is in our field of vision. The way we read is greatly dependent on many things we bring with us

---

23 Harry Lee Poe, *Christian Witness in a Postmodern World* (Nashville: Abingdon, 2000), 122.

Wonder Where the Wonder Went

in our backgrounds, culture, education, prejudices, perspectives, and general attitude. The same is true for what we see. The frame of mind as one looks out through prison bars largely determines whether we see mud or stars.

From an unknown author comes the perfect prayer for the closing of this chapter:

> O God, we thank you for this day. Open our eyes that we may let none of its wonders pass unseen. Amen.

QUESTIONS FOR REFLECTION AND CONVERSATION

1. Have you thought of any ways in which your visual acuity might be improved?
2. What are some of the times in which you have discovered wonder in the ordinary?
3. Have you ever been surprised by some experience of God grace and love in a most unexpected place?

BE QUICK TO OFFER PRAISE AND THANKSGIVING

SETTING THE STAGE

Praise the Lord!
Praise God in his sanctuary;
  praise him in his mighty firmament!
Praise him for his mighty deeds;
  praise him according to his surpassing greatness!
Praise him with trumpet sound;
  Praise him with lute and harp!
Praise him with tambourine and dance;
  praise him with strings and pipe!
Praise him with clanging cymbals;
  praise him with loud clashing cymbals!
Let everything that breathes praise the Lord!
Praise the Lord!
                    — Psalm 150

This is definitely a no-holds-barred call to praise. It literally pulls out all the stops. The only time most of us come close to this kind of free-for-all turning loose is at a ball game! There is a little of the flavor of modern sporting events in this psalm when we see the call for clanging cymbals with the addition that they be loud clashing cymbals. Doesn't this remind you of the never-ending call from the cheerleaders to "get louder"? The fact that we don't feel as free in worship to express our emotions as we do at a ballgame is a discussion outside the perimeters of this book. (I get into enough trouble discussing religion, I refuse to take on sports or politics!)

The cynic might be quick to assume that God needs a lot of praising. The bottom line is that we are the ones who need the praise-giving. That may be the reason, as many have observed, that in the Scriptures there are more calls to praise than there are calls to prayer. Psalm 136 provides the basic reason for our praise: *O give thanks to the Lord, for he is good, for his steadfast love endures forever* (136:1). The reader and the congregation both participated in the reading of this psalm with the phrase, *for his steadfast love endures forever,* repeated twenty-six times by those attending worship!

Since the Psalter is a prayer and hymn book, it was easy to sing this phrase all the way home. The central theme of God's covenant love in both the Hebrew and Christian scriptures can be summarized in this powerful phrase: *the steadfast love of the Lord endures forever.* That love and covenant faithfulness are tied together in Psalm 108:3-4:

> *I will give thanks to you, O Lord,*
>   *among the peoples,*
> *And I will sing praises to you*
>   *among the nations.*
> *For your steadfast love is higher than*
>   *the heavens,*
> *And your faithfulness reaches to*
>   *the clouds.*

Praise and thanksgiving are rooted in the basic message of grace that has always been God's overriding agenda when dealing with his wayward world. This morning, one of the closing prayers from a book I use as a part of my devotional time, gave me the same reminder:

> Lord, make me have perpetual love and reverence for your holy Name, for you never fail to help and govern those whom you have set upon the sure foundation of your loving-kindness through Jesus Christ our Lord, who lives and reigns with you and the Holy Spirit, one God, for ever and ever. Amen.[24]

REFLECTIONS

> Maybe I shouldn't grumble so much. I should just work harder at making sure every day is worth living. Or at least every other day. There have to be rest days too.[25]

> Edward taped a piece of paper onto one of the tables downstairs that says, "Please, no ORGAN RECITALS at this table." [26]

Both of these quotes come from a delightful book written by a resident of a retirement home in Amsterdam. Henrik is far from a chronic complainer; he is constantly devising ways to live and enjoy life under the limitations of aging. He and his friend Edward aren't the only ones who don't want to hear "organ recitals" (litanies of health ailments) as the main course in every meal. It is really a laugh-out-loud book on many pages and, on the back cover, one reviewer writes: "When I'm an old man, I want to be Hendrik Groen."

Praise and thanksgiving are the best antidotes to griping and complaining about all that is wrong with the world and almost everybody in it. During the Great Depression one of the popular songs was *"Keep on the Sunny Side"*:

---

24 Phyllis Tickle, *The Divine Hours: Prayers for Summertime* (New York; Doubleday, 2000), 126.
25 Henrik Groen, *The Secret Diary of Henrik Groen* (New York: Grand Central Publishing, 2014), 140.
26 Ibid, 298.

Oh, the storm and its fury broke today,
Crushing hopes that we cherish so dear.
Clouds and storms will in time pass away.
The sun again will shine bright and clear.
Keep on the sunny side, always on the sunny side,
Keep on the sunny side of life.
It will help us every day, it will brighten all the way,
If you keep on the sunny side of life.

It is all too obvious that if you spend your time dwelling on the negative aspects of life in this world, you will not be finding much of its wonder. If you are able to "count your blessings" and every day spot new things (and people) for which to be grateful, wonders of life will unfold that go undetected by those who only know how to give "organ recitals." One writer gives this prescription: "Some of the types of food for the soul: gratitude, simplicity, a listening spirit, appreciation of one's vulnerability, recognition of the fragility of life, scripture, unceasing prayer."[27] Gratitude is his first recommended food for soul-nourishment. Robert Wicks puts gratitude in a larger context:

> True humility helps us let go of our sense of entitlement, rejoice, and be grateful for all material and personal gifts we have been given in life — especially the gift of who we are.[28]

When we are able to get rid of the burdens of entitlement and recognize that everything in life is really gift, we have set ourselves free to be grateful for every good thing that comes our way. Paul even learned to be grateful for things that didn't at first appear to have any blessing attached to them. The word *grace* basically means gift; God's grace is not deserved or earned in any way but is given because of who God is and not because of who we are. When we can begin seeing each day as a gift (and I assure you, more and more of that is done with increasing age), you find yourself able to appreciate many more of the wonders of existence.

---

27 Robert J. Wicks, *Crossing the Desert,* 109.
28 Ibid, 76.

Beginning this section with Psalm 150 may seem the thing most appropriate when "God is in his heaven, and all is right with the world." We need to remember that the Psalms in their present form were collected at the time of the Babylonian exile when both Jerusalem and the Temple lay in ruins. When their captors asked for some of the songs the people used to sing in their native land, the people responded with one accord: *"How can we sing the Lord's song in a strange land?"* (Psalm 137:4). We need to remember:

> Paradoxically, the people who found it unthinkable to sing the Lord's song in a strange land may have found that actually singing these songs (and writing new ones) was one of the few things that kept them sane and gave them hope. That they formed the basic hymnbook of the second Temple in Jerusalem…as well as the thousands of local Jewish gatherings in "synagogues" around the world and in the holy land itself, we should have no doubt.[29]

Knowing that the people who sang *"the steadfast love of the Lord endures forever"* did so as exiles in Babylon, reminds me of those who sang *"Keep on the sunny side"* in the midst of economic catastrophe. But in the case of the exiles, their reason for singing was the conviction that even in this foreign land, God had not abandoned them. His faithfulness and loving-kindness gave them a reason to sing. Gratitude and a thankful spirit change everything and sometimes for everybody. Mother Teresa provides such an example:

> One evening we went out and we picked up four people from the street. And one of them was in a most terrible condition. I told the Sisters: "You take care of the other three; I will take care of the one who looks worse." So, I did for her all that my love can do. I put her in bed, and there was such a beautiful smile on her face. She took hold of my hands, as she said one word only: "Thank you" — and then she died.[30]

---

29 N. T. Wright, *The Case for the Psalms*, 9-10.
30 Mother Teresa, *The Joy in Loving* (New York: Viking, 1996), 176.

EXCURSUS

> The saints were masterful at taking the ordinary, everyday events of life and turning them into holy moments.[31]

> Like any good poem, the purpose of this one (Proverbs 31) is to draw attention to the often-overlooked glory of the everyday.[32]

Proverbs 31 has a challenging question: *A wife of noble character who can find? (TNIV), Who can find a virtuous woman? (KJV),* or *A capable wife who can find? (NRSV).* The reply you want to give to the question (if you read the description for such a wife) is, "No one!" This woman puts Martha in the shade and relegates her to a dawdler! It appears more like a recipe for a nervous breakdown than it does a capable or faithful wife. She does everything — and more! Rachel Held Evans opines: "The poem closely resembles the characteristics of a heroic poem celebrating the exploits of a warrior."[33] She then gives an insight that makes far more sense than seeing this as a job description. (And we need to remember: it is a poem!) Instead of seeing this passage prescriptively as a command to women she sees it as an ode to women.[34] Here is her thesis:

> I looked into this, and sure enough, in Jewish culture it is not the women who memorize Proverbs 31 but the men. Husbands commit each line of the poem to memory, so they can recite it to their wives at the Sabbath meal, usually in a song.....We turned an anthem into an assignment, a poem into a job description.[35]

Wonder what kind of wonders this produced and would produce today if men adopted this custom? Aside from wives fainting

---

31 Matthew Kelly, *Rediscover the Saints* (North Palm Beach: Blue Sparrow, 2019), 10.
32 Rachel Held Evans, *A Year of Biblical Womanhood* (Nashville: Nelson Books, 2012), 76.
33 Ibid, 75.
34 Ibid, 77-78.
35 Ibid, 88-89.

from surprise and wonder themselves, it would create an entirely new dimension of affirmation.

SUMMATION

"Why what is it to live? Not to eat and drink and breathe — but to feel the life on you down all the fibers of being, passionately and joyfully." (From *The Letters of Robert Browning and Elizabeth*).

> Standing outside we saw sinister clouds glowing in the west and the whole sky alive with clouds of ever-changing shapes and colors, from steel blue to blood red. The desolate grey mud huts provided a sharp contrast, while the puddles on the muddy ground reflected the glowing sky. Then, after minutes of moving silence, one prisoner said to another, "How beautiful the world *could* be!"[36]

We are not surprised to read such a romantic statement from the correspondence between Robert Browning and Elizabeth. If you don't know the source of the second above account, you are much surprised to realize the episode took place in a Nazi concentration camp during WWII. To suggest that praise and thanksgiving can bring a new dimension to life, even in a death camp, is to suggest that how much wonder we find in life, how much we find for which to be grateful, depends on us and not on our circumstances.

It is entirely too human and too easy to allow the things that come our way to shape the way we will come at life. "I am the master of my fate; I am the captain of my soul" *is* true in the sense that we are the determiners of what we make out of life. The people who have inspired me have been those who did not allow the blows and disappointments of life to relegate them to a life of misery and unhappiness. Lincoln is reported to have said, "Most people are about as happy as they make up their minds to be." I wouldn't want to push the envelope quite that far but I would say that we

---

36 Victor Frankl, *Man's Search for Meaning* (Boston: Beacon Press, 1959), 39.

are responsible for our own happiness and that happiness is always a by-product of living for more than simply oneself.

A personal sidebar: The prayer I cited earlier from the devotional book I read each morning is also filled with Scripture readings that include large chunks of the Psalms. There is something I have found, at the suggestion of several writers, that has greatly increased my understanding and the Impact these readings have made on me. I read the selections aloud. Try it. It makes all the difference in the world to hear the words in your own voice as well as see the text.

QUESTIONS FOR REFLECTION AND CONVERSATION

1. What do you think it means when we find more calls to praise than prayer in the Bible?
2. Why do you believe it is easy to grumble and give "organ recitals" as we get older? Are there remedies for reducing this tendency?
3. What do you think of Rachel Held Evan's interpretation of Proverbs 31?

5
READ, READ, READ — WRITE, WRITE, WRITE

SETTING THE STAGE

> *Your word is a lamp to my feet*
> *and a light to my path*
> —(Psalm 119:105).

I cannot imagine what life would be like without the words of Holy Scripture. When I was sixteen and preached my first sermon in a Youth Week at my home church, I owned a *Thompson Chain Reference Bible*[37] and *Cruden's Complete Concordance.*[38] The Bible has maps, charts, cross-references, a subject index and all kinds of study aids and the concordance leaves no English biblical word forsaken. With these two sermonic aids, I preached up a storm — with a lot of wind, hail, and lightning. What I lacked in knowledge I made up for with passion and enthusiasm. I wish I had saved those early sermons but not having done so has probably saved me lots of regret.

---

37 Frank Charles Thompson, ed., *The New Chain-Reference Bible.* Third Improved Edition (Indianapolis: B.B. Kirkbridge Bible Co., 1934).
38 Alexander Cruden, *Cruden's Complete Concordance to the Old and New Testaments* (Philadelphia: The John C. Winston Company, 1949).

My collection of Bibles now includes some of my recommendations for a basic library: *The New Revised Standard Bible*,[39] *The New Living Translation*,[40] (not the *Living Bible* which is not my recommended paraphrase), *The Message* by Eugene Peterson,[41] *(which is an excellent paraphrase), Today's New International Version*,[42] *The New Jerusalem Bible*,[43] *The New Testament in Modern English* translated by J. B. Phillips,[44] *The New King James Version*,[45] and the Revised English Bible.[46] There are other translations I also find helpful, especially *The New Testament, An Expanded Translation* by Kenneth Wuest.[47] It provides verb tenses often neglected in other translations. For example, most versions translate Matthew 7:7: *Ask, and it will be given you;* Wuest's translation: *Keep on asking for something and it will be given you.*

Whenever I am asked my recommendation for the "best" translation, my reply is always the same: "The one you will read." I don't think any of the basic translations will lead you astray. Some are easier to understand than others and in one church where I was interim, I secured multiple copies of *Today's Living Translation* which we used in a Bible study. At the conclusion of my work there, one member thanked me for supplying him with a Bible he could understand and enjoy reading.

Nothing takes the place of reading the words of Scripture. The only preliminary help I find necessary is one that enables me to understand the context in which the passage was written, to whom and why it was written, and the form in which is appears (poetry,

---

39 *New Revised Standard Bible* (Grand Rapids: Zondervan Publishing House, 1989).
40 *New Living Translation* (New York: American Bible Society, 1996).
41 Eugene Peterson, *The Message* (Colorado Springs: Navpress, 2002).
42 *Today's New International Version* (Grand Rapids: Zondervan, 2005).
43 *New Jerusalem Bible* (New York: Doubleday, 1985).
44 J. B. Phillips, *The New Testament in Modern English* (New York: The Macmillan Company, 1985).
45 *New King James Version* (Nashville: Thomas Nelson Publishers, 1982).
46 *Revised English Bible* (Oxford: Oxford University Press, 1989).
47 Kenneth S. Wuest, *The New Testament, An Expanded Translation* (Grand Rapids: William B. Eerdman's Publishing Company, 1961).

wisdom literature, etc.) A basic book I recommend is *Theological Bible Commentary,* edited by Gail R. O'Day and David L. Peterson.[48] It is concise and readable and supplies almost everything one needs to read the text with an educated perspective.

REFLECTIONS

> Calvin Miller: "John and Sophie taught me that it is not enough to believe in something sincerely. It is also important to be informed."[49]
>
> Matthew Kelly: "For years I have been encouraging people to read five pages of a great spiritual book each day.[50]

I cannot imagine what life would be like without books. Books have been the "tools" in my life from the earliest days. My father was an avid reader and during his leisure hours I hardly ever remember him without a book in his hands. The depression deprived him of a completed education, but he was determined to continue that education on his own.

I agree with Calvin Miller that sincerity in belief is not sufficient; it is also important and absolutely necessary to be informed. In a heated discussion in a group meeting about an issue that is not relevant to our discussion, one of the participants finally exclaimed in frustration, "Well, I believe it simply because I believe it." In another book I noted that Jesus made an addition to Scripture when asked which was the greatest commandment of the Law. Jesus cites Deuteronomy 6:5: *You must love Yahweh your God with all your heart, with all your soul, and with all your strength* (NJB). He quotes it differently: *You must love the Lord your God with all your heart, with all your soul, and with all your mind. This is the first and greatest commandment* (Matthew 22:37, NJB).

---

48 Gail R. O'Day and David L. Peterson, eds., *Theological Bible Commentary* (Louisville: Westminster John Knox Press, 2009).
49 Calvin Miller, *Life is Mostly Edges* (Nashville: Thomas Nelson, 2008), 155.
50 Matthew Kelly, *Rediscover the Saints,* 110.

I purposely chose *The New Jerusalem Bible* for its translation because of the use of Yahweh instead of the usually English, *You shall love the Lord your God*. In the Hebrew Scriptures, whenever the God's name is used it appears as YHWH and is so sacred that it is never spoken. Adonai is usually the preferred substitution. No one knows exactly how YHWH is to be pronounced because the Hebrew text contains no vowels. In the Genesis 1 version of creation, the text reads: *In the beginning God….*In the Genesis 2 version, the text reads: *Yahweh God said…* When Moses encounters God at the burning bush, the text reads: *When Yahweh saw him going across to look* (Exodus 3:4). Yahweh is the sacred, personal, relational, covenant name of God. You don't have to know all this to understand the Hebrew Scriptures but it certainly makes your reading a little more informed.

Which brings me to my mental response when someone says, "Well, that is what I believe": "And you have come to that based on what?" Most often it is not spoken because it is perceived as too challenging, and it is. I have taken seriously the admonition to a young minister (and meant for everyone) in II Timothy 2:15 — *Study to shew thyself approved unto God, a workman that needeth not to be ashamed, rightly dividing the word of truth* (KJV). A more contemporary translation that remains true to the Greek is: *Make every effort to present yourself before God as a proven worker who has no need to be ashamed, but who keeps the message of truth on a straight path* (NJB). Summary: be an educated minister; know whereof you speak and when you don't know, don't speak.

That means my reading must be very broad, dealing with many subjects other than theology. The best recommendation I ever received before I began my college education was, "Don't major in Bible. Get a liberal arts education." So, when I attended Georgetown College in Kentucky, I was a Biology major with an English minor. When people asked what I was studying as an undergraduate, their response to my answer was usually one word: "What?!" I found that education especially helpful in the years which followed with the on-going battle between science and religion. My thesis remains the same: there is no real conflict between true science and true religion. That is a matter for another book which I'm not sure I will ever write. Southern Seminary and post-graduate work at Southeastern Seminary provided me with the necessary tools and motivation to keep the message of truth on a straight line, or at least as straight as I can make it.

EXCURSUS

> Altogether, I think we ought to read only books that bite and sting us. If the book we are reading doesn't shake us awake like a blow on the skull, why bother reading it in the first place? So that it can make us happy, as you put it? Good God, we'd be just as happy if we had no books at all; books that make us happy we could, in a pinch, also write ourselves. A book must be the axe for the frozen sea within us. That is what I believe.[51]

The above correlates with my oft repeated: "Never read a book you could have written yourself. Never read a book someone wrote while standing in line at the post office." Read books written by people who have credentials to make them reliable sources for the information and ideas they are presenting. Read books by persons who have done their homework and the research shows it. Read as many primary sources as possible and in the original language if you are able. But above all, read books that are worth reading. Books that will expand your horizons and challenge you to do some reflecting and rethinking.

For some people this is often seen as a problem because they fear they might lose their faith. I don't consider that the challenging reading I have done in the past has diminished any of my faith; I feel it is wider, stronger, and more truly biblical than it has ever been. It is also more inclusive, which does not mean I have forsaken the "basics" of Christian belief. I have made much more room at the Lord's table than was provided by my boyhood pastor

---

51 Nancy Malone, *Walking a Literary Labyrinth* (New York: Riverhead Books), 117-118.

who, before communion, would invite those not members of our church to leave. I didn't really know this was "closed communion" brought to us through the courtesy of Landmark Baptists.

I certainly don't ask others to believe everything I do (although I see myself as biblically and theologically orthodox), only that we be willing to listen to each other's life stories and the pilgrimages that have brought us to this place in our lives. Historically, Baptists were those who granted the right of fellowship across honest differences of opinion. The confession that held us together and created our community was: "Jesus Christ is Lord."

In one of my interim churches, I recommended Doug Marlette's *The Bridge*[52] as a book I wanted to give as a gift to the church library. The librarian didn't know the book and wanted to check it out. She did and informed me it was not suitable material for the library. The author was known to me through the Pulitzer Prize-winning *Kudzu* comic strips with the infamous Rev. Will B. Done helping to provide much needed comic relief in an overly-serious culture. On the back cover, Robert Coles writes: "The other novelists who started out as cartoonists — John Updike, Eudora Welty, and Flannery O'Connor come to mind — he entertains so thoroughly while doing so that his moral and human truths slip up on us without our ever noticing."

The rejection did not prevent my using one of the episodes from the book in a sermon. Pick Cantrell is having a real problem with his grandmother and asks for advice:

I shook my head. "This family is like living in a lunatic asylum. What should I do? Tell me what to do. I'll do it."

"…I don't know. I don't give advice. My advice is not to ever give advice or take it." Buzz dragged his spoon through his chili and said, "But if you're asking me what might smooth things over and get you back on track with the rest of the family I'd say just make a trip over and apologize."

"Why doesn't she apologize?"

---

52 Doug Marlette, *The Bridge* (New York: HarperCollins, 2001).

"She can't. You know that. She's just one of those people lost in her righteousness. If anything's going to happen, you're going to have to instigate it. You're going to have to step up. Be the mature one."

"She always counts on other people's maturity. But I'm not mature, not this time."

"I can't do it, Buzz."

"Why not?"

"Because."

"Why?"

"Because" — I felt silly uttering it — "if I do, she wins." "Pickard, son," said Buzz, smiling as he reached across the table and placed his hand on my shoulder, "you know as well as I do this ain't no contest."[53]

That seemed to be a sermon in itself.

SUMMATION

> A study by Yale University researchers several years ago showed a significant linkage between book reading and longevity. That's right, reading books leads to cognitive benefits that positively impact greater survival rates. Peter W. Marty.[54]

This is good news in the light of the T-shirt I saw on one occasion and failed to buy: "So Many Books….So Little Time." Although I don't think at 85 I'll ever live long enough to read all the books on my shelves (aside from the fact that I keep buying more), I always feel as though I have the world at my fingertips and inspiration available at the flip of a page as I journey with a gifted writer. I am able to travel to places and have experiences I never thought would be mine. The joy of reading has certainly enhanced these days of restrictions due to COVID-19. I cannot

---

53 Ibid, 129-131.
54 *Christian Century.* May 20, 2020, 2.

imagine how impoverished I would feel without the enrichment of outstanding authors and outstanding books.

Personal sidebar: This week I stumbled across the ad for a sweatshirt I asked my wife to get me for my birthday. I think I might have the courage to wear it — on occasion. It reads:

> **That's
> What I Do.
> I Read.
> And I Know
> Things.**

I have not forgotten about the encouragement to write

My wife has always kept a journal (for her eyes only) and she cannot say enough about how valuable that has been. Her words are not for publication but it has been a personal satisfaction to see her own words on paper. We are so used to "talking it out" that we often forget the value of "writing it out." People used to write letters. I just finished viewing Ken Burns classic PBS series on the Civil War. One of the highlights was the reading of countless letters from soldiers to their loved ones. Many were profound, but all were amazing in the depths of emotions that were expressed in words that issued from heart and soul. How poorer we would be without a record of that correspondence. Sometimes I almost weep when I consider future generations looking back on this one and finding (if possible) tweets and texts with the special language that made them quicker to write. My advice: at least once a month write an extended note or letter to someone. The recipient will be the richer for it, but so will you.

"I didn't realize I felt that way until I just said it," is the confession from someone Kate Murphy records as involved in a conversation of really listening.[55] I believe this happens more often

---

55 Kate Murphy, *You're Not Listening*, 7.

as we let our thoughts flow out in written form. A broader understanding of many of the subjects I have tackled in my books came in the process of writing. Whether or not you want to call this inspiration is beside the point. It happens to most people who let writing become the free flow of ideas. For us talkers, it is at times a better way to do our reflection and contemplation; it helps us to stay focused. This kind of writing becomes a better way to know and understand ourselves.

If you need some solid scientific reasons for writing, this should do it:

> It is important to write about loss, loves, deaths, and personal failures. Do it for at least fifteen minutes a day. And guess what? The researchers report a variety of mental and physical benefits, including improved immune function, less emotional anxiety or depression, even quicker reemployment following job loss. Routinely writing about anything has been shown to improve memory capacity. Why does writing about a difficult time make you feel better? No one's altogether sure, though a long-standing theory holds that letting go on paper lessens inhibition, inhibition being a source of stress.[56]

If you feel you have an article or a book in you, go for it. When people plead that they don't know how, I make the following suggestions: Schedule a certain time each day to write. Go to a special "writing place" that offers no, or few, distractions and pull up that blank screen or open that notebook to a blank page.

Don't wait for inspiration, just sit there until something comes to you and begin to write. When I do the first draft of a book, I just let it fly; editing is for a later time. I'm not worried about spelling or punctuation or even sense at the moment. Just getting my thoughts out on the page is what counts. Write what you care about. Write what your worries and anxieties are right now. Write about things that really matter to you. Who knows what may come from what you write? Something has already come from it because you have gotten it out on a page.

---

56 Lee Eisenberg, *The Point Is* (New York: Twelve, 2016), 52-53.

My final advice: Read, read, read! Write, write, write! You'll be amazed at what your discipline and your efforts produce and you may even experience a little wonder along the way.

QUESTIONS FOR REFLECTION AND CONVERSATION

1. Did you find anything especially helpful in the section on Bible reading?
2. What books have you read that had a bite and sting about them but that you wouldn't have missed for the world?
3. What reading and writing habits have you developed and how would you like to improve or broaden them?

Stay off the Defensive and the Critical

SETTING THE STAGE

>*Refrain from anger and turn from wrath; do not fret — it leads only to evil.* (Psalm 37:8, TNIV).
>
>*But the people were thirsty for water there and they grumbled against Moses. They said, "Why did you bring us up out of Egypt to make us and our children and livestock die of thirst?" Then Moses cried out to the Lord, "What am I to do with these people? They are almost ready to stone me."* (Exodus 17:3-4, TNIV).

The KJV translates "grumbled" as "murmured." I've always liked that translation because you can almost feel and hear it all the way through the wilderness experience of God's people. "Murmur, murmur, murmur" is the on-going complaining and discontent the people have for the journey they had assumed was to a land flowing with milk and honey. Moses becomes the brunt of the grumbling they are fearful of addressing to God. At one point, things get so bad that some in the group suggest they get rid of Moses, choose a new leader, and go back to Egypt. How could they so quickly have forgotten 400 years of slavery in which they were constantly calling out to God for deliverance? Answer: this was not exactly what they thought deliverance would look like.

Constant fretting and dissatisfaction with present circumstances is not conducive to happiness and may even lead (as the psalmist suggests) to evil. I don't hear much praise and thanksgiving coming from the lips of the Exodus people as they take steps of freedom to a new life. They even get tired of the manna God provides when it turns out to be the daily bill of fare. We wonder why they could not have been so grateful for their release from captivity that they would have been grateful for whatever God provided.

A major purpose of such biblical accounts is for us to be able to see ourselves. In being a pastor, it is so easy to see oneself leading a group of people who respond just like Moses' congregation. It is so easy to grumble because of the grumblers, to fret because of the fretters, to murmur because of the murmurers, and to cry to the Lord when someone suggests that what they really need is a new leader. (And I assure you, I was no Moses!) The "evil" that comes from falling into this temptation is that one misses many of the wonders that are to be found in every congregation.

> Another year, and I still don't like old people. Their walker shuffle, their unreasonable impatience, their countless complaints, their tea and cookies, their bellyaching. Me? I am eighty-three years old.[57]
>
> Life in here (retirement home) consists of either *never* or *always*. One day the food is "*never* served on time and *always* too hot," and the next, "*always* too early and *never* hot enough."[58]
>
> I went downstairs for a cup of pea soup. It went down great, but I had to listen to at least ten stories about mothers and grandmothers whose pea soup was so much better. The past, they're always going on about the past. Live in the present for a change, you mummified nitwits![59]

---

57 Henrik Groen, *The Secret Diary of Henrik Groen*, 44.
58 Ibid, 5.
59 Ibid, 356.

Henry Groen's account of life in a retirement home in Amsterdam is hilarious, delightful, and full of wisdom for life in general. Living on the defensive (always ready to take offense if someone should challenge us) and with a critical spirit (nothing is ever exactly as it ought to be) are two of the best "wonder squelchers" I know. (There are others we'll mention later). Whether in a wilderness journey, a retirement or nursing home, or a COVID-19 world, wonders abound if we have the attitude, mindset, and perspective that enable us to experience them.

REFLECTIONS

> Focusing on the unfairness of circumstances keeps you comparing yourself with others rather than appreciating your own special uniqueness.[60]
>
> Whether human beings admit it or not, we are all in love with — even addicted to — the status quo and the past, even when it is killing us.[61]

These two ideas are appropriate commentaries on the thankless group it was Moses' responsibility to shepherd across the desert. When the cry came to go back to Egypt, eyebrows ought to have been raised by the more astute members of the group. That had bee a time and a place that was literally killing them and yet it looked so much better than their present reality. With more perceptive and reflective vision, many of us can become aware of our own addiction to the "good old days," rather than a commitment to live fully in the challenging present days. The past always looks so much better because it is fixed, it is over; we know it will not change from what it was, it is set in stone. There is nothing to be afraid of because it will never change. (Only our perception and remembrance of it!)

Moses' grumblers feared just what we all fear. They have been provided water at their present stop in the desert, but will there be

---

60 Cherie Carter-Scott, *If Life is a Game....Here are the Rules,* 38.
61 Richard Rohr, *Immortal Diamond,* xi.

water at the next stop? They are okay today but what about the long journey that is ahead? So much is unknown (as the future always is when we are brave enough to admit it). The cry to go back to what was known was, of course, impossible. It no longer existed. Shortly after we moved back to Louisville, I decided to go for a ride to the place where I had grown up. Nothing looked the same because nothing was the same. There was no way I could re-enter that time and continue my life exactly where I had left off twenty-five years earlier.

My older son had a plaque in his office with five simple words: "It Is What It Is." If I intend to live, I have to live in the present as it is. This is my calling. This is my challenge. This is my responsibility. One of my biblical heroes is Gideon, mainly because he is so real, so human. When an angel of the Lord appears to Gideon with the greeting, "*The Lord is with you, mighty warrior,*" Gideon appropriately responds: "*If the Lord is with us, why has all this happened to us?*" (Judges 6:12-13, TNIV). The scene of this encounter is a winepress, where Gideon is threshing out wheat; to thresh it out in the open was an invitation for the Midianites to take it. They were the marauders who had taken just about everything else. Such dire circumstances didn't seem to give any indication of God's presence. The conclusion of the conversation finds Gideon charged with the responsibility of stopping the Midianites. As with Esther, Gideon has a role to play for such a time as this. The past offers no opportunity for our involvement, it is only in the present moment with all of its "isness" that we find our place of responsibility and our call to duty. Meaning, of course, this is the place where we will find meaning and wonder.

Comparing ourselves with others only robs us of the opportunity to recognizie our significance in the place and time of our situation. Bemoaning the greater gifts and blessings of others is another formula for the diminishment of gratitude and thanksgiving for what has been given to us. Our focus belongs on what is in our treasure of "givenness," regardless of its size. Our circumstances may be limited and our gifts may appear to be few in number,

Wonder Where the Wonder Went

but these always provide the setting and the assets for us to fulfill God's calling.

EXCURSUS

> *Stop judging others, and you will not be judged. For others will treat you as you treat them. Whatever measure you use in judging others, it will be used to measure how you are judged. And why worry about a speck in a friend's eye when you have a log in your own?* (Matthew 7:1-3, NLT).
>
> *…the fruit of the Spirit is love, joy, peace, patience, kindness, goodness, faithfulness, gentleness and self-control* (Galatians 5:22, TNIV).

The major lesson from Matthew 7 is simple: if you're looking for specks, you'll never see wonders. What Jesus is talking about is not the discrimination that is necessary to determine major issues or the necessity of assessing when behavior is either dangerous or destructive to healthy relationships. I believe what is being condemned is the judgmental attitude which is best exemplified by the Pharisees with whom Jesus had so much trouble.

> In a survey, more than 750 people (both Christians and non-Christians), were provided the prompt: "Christians are…" and offered about two dozen adjectives. The number one answer, selected by Christians and non-Christians alike, was "judgmental."[62]

The above survey reflects what I believe Jesus is warning against in this section of the Sermon on the Mount. Through the years, I found too many Christians who believed their calling was to be part of the Holy Private Eye which was always on the lookout for something on which to stick a warning label. They were not on the lookout for God's wonders; they were on the lookout for anything they interpreted to be on God's forbidden list. Too many (as the survey indicated) have been "turned off" by this type of church

---

62 Christian Platt, *Post Christian* (New York: Jericho Books, 2014), 39.

and believe that all churches are the same. Why didn't the survey produce a large number of persons who could say: "Christians are loving, joyful, peace makers, patient, kind, attractively good, gentle and marked by self-control"?

Billy Graham said what I believe is the basic biblical principle: "It is the Holy Spirit's job to convict, God's job to judge, and my job to love."[63] John 16:8 promised that the Spirit *will convince the world of sin...*(NLT). Judgmental Christians have made themselves feel good because they fulfilled a "prophetic" role; unfortunately, their condemnation does not usually result in many changed lives. Question: how much has the judgment and condemnation from others encouraged and helped us to change? Usually, it only puts up our defenses and hardens us against the kind of gospel being presented.

We may never have thought being judgmental quite the way Henri Nouwen presents it:

> Imagine your having no need at all to judge anybody. Imagine your having no desire to decide whether someone is a good or bad person. Imagine your being completely free from the feeling that you have to make up your mind about the morality of someone's behavior. Imagine you could say, "I am judging no one!" Imagine — Wouldn't that be true inner freedom? The desert fathers from the fourth century said: "Judgment of others is a heavy burden."[64]

I imagine that would be quite a wonder to behold — in others, and particularly in ourselves.

SUMMATION

Julia Roller, my editor at HarperSanFrancisco, echoed what others have told me — namely, that unlike many post-

---

63 Rachel Held Evans, *Searching for Sunday,* 94.
64 Henri Nouwen, *The Mystery and the Passion* (Minneapolis: Fortress Press, 1992), 46.

modern Christians, I "write with a lack of anger." I hope that is true. Tom Steff.[65]

During the first of two government shutdowns in 2018, Maine senator Susan Collins presented a colorful talking stick to colleagues assembled in her office for bipartisan budget negotiations, hoping to inject some civility into the proceedings…Only the holder of the stick can speak while everyone else listens. But in Collin's office, it wasn't long before one senator had hurled the stick at another senator, chipping a glass elephant on her shelf.[66]

Perhaps another senator wasn't listening and the speaker just wanted to get his attention! The real tragedy of this episode is that most people would say, "Typical of how things work in Washington!" A few pages later in her book, the author of that episode provides this bit of research wisdom: "The truth is, we only become secure in our convictions by allowing them to be challenged."[67] Instead of rising blood pressure, rapid breathing, and an increased heartbeat, opposition ought to bring calm questions from us so we can fully understand the position of the other person. I fully agree that the more secure we are in our convictions the less need there will be for emotional or irrational outbursts — or the throwing of the talking stick!

What many have begun to see is that you need to have a non-dualistic, non-angry, and non-argumentative mind to process the really big issues with any depth or honesty, and most of us have not been effectively taught how to do that in practice. We were largely taught what to believe instead of how to believe.[68]

The discovery of larger truth and the appreciation of people with other points of view only come when our minds have a healthy

---

65 Tom Steff, *A Faith Worth Believing* (New York: HarperSanFrancisco, 2004), 17.
66 Kate Murphy, *You're Not Listening*, 80.
67 Ibid, 83.
68 Richard Rohr, *The Universal Christ* (New York: Convergent, 2019), 207.

way of believing. If a challenge to what we believe will bring our convictions down like a house of cards, this is the call to examine our convictions.

QUESTIONS FOR REFLECTION AND CONVERSATION

1. Do you believe that their grumbling and murmuring prevented the freed slaves from experiencing all the wonders of the Exodus experience?
2. How do you think being judgmental prevents us from hearing, seeing, and experiencing the wonders God and his people are working in his world?
3. How to you respond to Billy Graham's statement that "it is the Holy Spirit's job to convict, God's job to judge, and my job to love"?

Get Into Trouble the Way Jesus Did

Setting the Stage

> As he was walking along, (Jesus) saw Levi son of Alphaeus sitting at the tax booth, and he said to him, "Follow me." And he got up and followed him.
>
> And as he sat at dinner in Levi's house, many tax collectors and sinners were also sitting with Jesus and his disciples — for there were many who followed him. When the scribes of the Pharisees saw that he was eating with sinners and tax collectors, they said to his disciples, "Why does he eat with tax collectors and sinners?" (Mark 2:14-16).

Does your religion spend much of its time defining and deciding who cannot participate?[69]

What really got Jesus into trouble (and what the early church had to struggle with) was the question of who was welcome to participate in the fellowship of believers. Mark's incident takes place at a banquet given by Levi in response to his being called to be one of Jesus' disciples. Tax collectors were despised for two reasons: they were in the employ of the Roman Empire and they often

---

69 Richard Rohr, *The Immortal Diamond*, 109.

charged the people far more than they were required to turn over to the authorities. They were labelled "unclean" and were barred from Temple worship. "Sinners" were those who did not have the time or the inclination to keep all the 613 laws the scribes and Pharisees prided themselves on obeying. Here was Jesus, early in his ministry, reclining (as was the normal for dining) with a whole group of the wrong kind of people. Did he not realize what this would do to his image? Yes, he did.

Richard Rohr suggests that the problem of exclusion continues to be an issue with the church today. Although the specifics have changed, the principle remains the same: a place at the Lord's Table is frequently not open to all. Restrictions apply, depending on the location of the church, the creeds accepted as binding, and the social demands of the day. Jesus appears to have violated many of the religiously established boundaries of his day; he blatantly and deliberately colored outside the lines. He just couldn't seem to find anyone who was outside the reach of God's mercy, grace, and love. He just couldn't seem to find an "outsider."

To be with the "in" group always presents special hazards. In Mark 9:38, John tells Jesus: "*Teacher, we saw a man using your name to cast out demons, but we told him to stop because he isn't one of our group.*" Exorcists were common in that day and John appears to have witnessed an effective one working in the name of Jesus. But because he wasn't "one of our group," John didn't feel he was qualified to use Jesus' name. Jesus' reply to John was forceful and to the point: *"Don't stop him!"* A basic question: if people aren't doing things the way we do them, are they doing the Lord's work?

> The gospel of Luke claims that there were seventy-two disciples in all (10:1-2), including women, some of whom, in defiance of tradition are actually named in the New Testament: Joanna, the wife of Herod's steward, Chuza; Mary the mother of James and Joseph; Mary, the wife of Clopas; Susanna; Salome; and perhaps most famous of all, Mary from Magdala, whom Jesus had cured of "seven demons" (8:2). That these women functioned as Jesus' disciples is demonstrated by the

fact that all four gospels present them as travelling with Jesus from town to town (Mark 15:40-41; Matthew 27:55-56; Luke 8:2-3; 23:49; John 19:25). The gospels claim "many other women...followed (Jesus) and served him," too (Mark 15:40-41), from his first days preaching in Galilee to his last breath on the hill in Golgotha.[70]

The uproar over whether or not women can participate in church-life in the role of minster has largely been settled for many of us, but there continue to be some major exceptions. The above paragraph graphically illustrates the way women were regarded by Jesus in relation to his ministry and the roles assigned. It is even noted that some of these women supported financially the work of this disciple band. Other teachers no doubt followed similar procedures but on a smaller and far less demonstrative way.

The inclusion of tax collectors and women was only the beginning of what eventually got Jesus into a whole lot of trouble. His first sermon at the synagogue in Nazareth left the people amazed at the wisdom of his teaching until he opened the gospel doors too wide (Luke 4:16-30). As Jesus began to expand on the text he chose for the day (Isaiah 61), he gave two illustrations that did more than bring down the house; it got him thrown out of the house. He mentioned Elijah and Elisha who, instead of helping Israelites, many of whom needed their help, performed wonders for two foreigners (a widow of Zarephath and Naaman, a Syrian).

The reaction of the crowd was a move from cheering to violence:

> *When they heard this the people in the synagogue were furious. Jumping up, they mobbed him, and took him to the edge of the hill on which the city was built. They intended to push him over the cliff, but he slipped away through the crowd and left them* (Luke 4:28-30, NLT).

It is regrettable that most of us are able to remember times, perhaps not quite so violent, when people rose up in arms because

---

70   Reza Aslan, *Zealot*, 97.

someone wanted to include in the church fellowship people who "are not like us." I have lived during a time when segregation was a part of the culture and "those people" were okay as long as they "knew their place." I think Mother Teresa spoke to the issue in the most biblical way I have ever heard:

> When I went to China, I was asked, "What is a communist to you?" And I said: A child of God, my brother and my sister. And nobody had another word to say. There was perfect silence. And it was true, because the same loving hand created you, created me, created the man on the street.[71]

I can almost hear: "What will come next? That God loves all the people of all nations equally? That God loves others as much as he loves me? That John 3:16 is total in its inclusivity?" I am reminded of the bumper sticker I once saw: "Jesus loves you. But I'm his favorite." Perhaps a little bit of humor can take the sting out of the biblical challenge of an open table that even the early church had a problem with when the gospel message was extended to the Gentiles. I challenge you to read all four Gospels and make notes of the times (with specifics) when Jesus extends the gospel to the "unacceptable." He finds no one who is unacceptable to receive God's grace and love. He finds no one who is ineligible for inclusion at the Lord's table.

The absurdity of such divisions is illustrated by the classic line from the *Titanic* movie in which one of the "elite" women, before getting into a lifeboat asks, "Will the lifeboats be segregated according to class?" A major tragedy of the sinking of the unsinkable ship was that most of the third-class passengers perished. In God's Kingdom, nobody is third class. Everybody is first class simply because of having been created in the image of God.

The old song, "I've got a mansion just over the hilltop," disturbed me because I always felt more qualified for the accommodation mentioned in another song: "It's only a shanty in old shanty town, a tumble-down shack by an old railroad track." My

---

71 Mother Teresa, *The Joy in Loving*, 190.

worries were alleviated when a better translation of John 14 has Jesus announcing that there are *many rooms in the Father's house.* He never indicates that some will be executive suites. Gradations in accommodation would reflect the kingdoms of this world, not the Kingdom of God.

EXCURSUS

The love for equals is a human thing — of friend for friend, brother for brother. It is to love what is loving and lovely. The world smiles.

The love for the less fortunate is a beautiful thing — the love for those who suffer, for those who are poor, the sick, the failures, the unlovely. This is compassion, and it touches the heart of the world.

The love for the more fortunate is a rare thing — to love those who succeed where we fail, to rejoice without envy with those who rejoice, the love of the poor for the rich, of the black man for the white man. The world is always bewildered by its saints.

> And then there is the love for the enemy — love for the one who does not love you but mocks, threatens, and inflicts pain. The tortured's love for the torturer. This is God's love. It conquers the world.[72]

In the Sermon on the Mount (Matthew 5:38-48), when Jesus commands us to love our enemies, that love is coupled with the instruction to do good to those who intentionally do bad to us. It's probably the most difficult, and the most neglected, of Jesus' teaching. The key, of course, is to base it on the kind of love that Paul describes in I Corinthians 13. That love has nothing to do with emotions; it is all about our actions. This kind of love really is greater than faith and hope. It really is the only thing that conquers the world. It is the love than encompasses all humankind and is always ready to pull up another chair to the table of God's fellowshipping community.

---

72 Frederick Buechner, *Listening to Your Life,* 302-303.

You can see why Jesus got into so much trouble. He flung open the doors of his Father's house and issued a blanket invitation. It was simply too much for many in his day. If we are honest, we find it really too much for many in our day - if you mean by putting it into practice.

> Galatians 3:28: *There is no longer Jew or Greek, there is no longer slave or free, there is no longer male and female; for all of you are one in Christ Jesus.*

We've been trying to figure out exactly how that applies to our daily lives ever since Paul wrote it. Jesus' ministry of grace, mercy, and love included those who were outside any congregation of faith. Most people have no idea what shock waves it sent through the crowd the day Jesus told the story of what it means to be a neighbor and the hero turned out to be a despised Samaritan (Luke 10:25-37). Aside from open mouths, shaking heads, and speechless tongues, there must have been more than a few who quietly slipped away from the crowd. We generally make the Gospels much too devotional as we read Jesus' parables with their insistence that his Kingdom is nothing like the kingdoms of this world. My comment: you can say that again!

SUMMATION

> Life is either a daring adventure or nothing at all. Helen Keller.[73]

My summation is quick and to the point. If you want life to be a daring adventure, just get into the kind of trouble Jesus got into and for the reasons he got into it. Yes, it will be trouble but I guarantee you will see wonders you never dreamed could happen and never would have happened without the Jesus' kind of trouble!

---

73 Cherie Carter-Scott, *If Life is a Game....Here are the Rules*, 123.

QUESTIONS FOR REFLECTION AND CONVERSATION

1. Do you agree with the author on the reasons Jesus got into so much trouble with the religious authorities?
2. Where have you found it difficult to be as inclusive as Jesus was?
3. What did you think of Mother Teresa's response to the question posed to her on her visit to China?

DETERMINE TO MAKE A DIFFERENCE IN YOUR WORLD

SETTING THE STAGE

> Criticism of Mother Teresa is often directed at the insignificant scale of the work she and the Sisters undertake by comparison with the need....But then Christianity is not a statistical view of life.[74]

When I first learned about this criticism of Mother Teresa's work in Calcutta, my immediate response was, "So the rule of thumb is: if we can't help on a grand scale, then we shouldn't help anybody? That certainly takes us off the hook for making any efforts toward helping those in need." Jesus must have wasted his time because he certainly didn't heal everyone in his brief ministry in a tiny corner of the world. Sometimes you need to dismiss criticism as simply ridiculous. Those who are into a statistical view of life will logically decide there really isn't much any of us can do.

What Mother Teresa did is what we all can do: she made a difference in her world. In another book, I posed the proverbial question as to whether it is better to be a big frog in a little pond or a little frog in a big pond. When I look at my life, I concluded

---

74 Malcolm Muggeridge, *Something Beautiful for God*, 28.

that I usually feel more like a frog in a puddle. My sphere of influence and my possible contributions appear to be so small and insignificant in the face of all the needs in our hurting world. My conclusion: the best that I can do, and what I am certain I am called to do, is to make a difference in my tiny piece of the world.

> *"Yet who knows whether you have come to the kingdom for such a time as this?"* (Esther 4:14, NKJV).

The question that Esther's uncle addressed to her is the question that is addressed to us regardless of our status or position in society. There is no place that does not provide some opportunity for service and ministry on a scale that we are able to offer. There is nothing more life-affirming and motivating than to wake up each day knowing: "God has put me in this place for such a moment as this. There is something I am called to do and can do. May I have the faith and courage of Esther to commit myself to the task which lies so plainly before me." Most of our spheres of influence and possibility are mere puddles in comparison to Esther's opportunity to save her people. Nowhere in Scripture do we find any indication that small deeds are insignificant or small places don't matter. A cup of cold water, the feeding of a hungry person, the visiting of someone in prison, and the providing of clothing to the needy are all noted by Jesus as significant services that are marked for eternal remembrance (Matthew 25:31-46).

Perhaps the most famous of all Mother Teresa's sayings is the way to complete setting the stage for this chapter: "We are not called to do great things. We are called to do small things with great love."

REFLECTIONS

> The response of Desmond Doss in the movie *Hacksaw Ridge* when asked what he will do when confronted by an enemy soldier getting ready to shoot him: "I don't have answers for questions that big."

The movie is difficult to watch because it shows one of the bloodiest battles of WWII at Okinawa, but the inspiring and incredible story is all the more memorable because of its authenticity. Desmond Doss volunteered to serve in the army as a medic, but refused to carry a rifle because it was against his religious convictions to take the life of another person. If this were not a true story you would dismiss it as unbelievable — and it is. Desmond Doss was the first in American history to receive the Medal of Honor without firing a shot.

The most inspiring scene for me comes after the second attempt to take the ridge on Okinawa. Those who were able, fled the ridge down the rock wall. Desmond is ready to make the same move when he pauses to pray: "I can't hear you anymore. I don't know what you want me to do!" At that moment, out of the darkness, come voices: "Medic! Help me, Lord!" At that point, the story shifts into what will later be termed a miracle. Desmond rescues one man at a time, letting them down by rope from the top of the ridge. His continuing prayer is, "Just one more, Lord. Let me get just one more." He saves 75 men.

The next day, before the charge that finally captures the ridge, the troops refuse to go into battle until Desmond prays for them. In the interviews with the real Desmond Doss, you meet a man who doesn't see himself as a great hero. He was simply an ordinary soldier who was doing his job as a medic.

The action of this one man in his place in the world at that time is nothing less than Wonder with a capital W. He was determined to make a difference in his world by living out the convictions he could not abandon and combining those convictions with the faith and courage to do what he felt called to do.

> Henri Nouwen: A courageous life, therefore, is a life lived from the center. It is a deeply rooted life, the opposite of a superficial life. "Have courage" therefore means, "Let your center speak."[75]

---

75 Henri J. Nouwen, *Bread for the Journey* (New York: HarperOne, 1997), July 26.

Desmond Doss certainly lived his life from the center. I believe Nouwen is correct in making this the way to live a courageous life. It is so easy to lead a superficial life, which is not so much bad, as it is irrelevant. Irrelevant to becoming the best version of yourself, and irrelevant when it comes to making a difference in your world. I hold it to be the greatest temptation we face. It is impossible to remember how many times I have heard discouraged people confess in one way or another, "After all, what difference can I make?" The answer: not much, until you muster the courage to get in touch with your center and do what you are obviously called to do.

It is easy to tell when the superficial takes over the center because I find myself thinking, "No. This is not who I really am." Whenever I took a statistical view of life and ministry, I knew I was in trouble. In the church world it is too easily concluded, "By the numbers you live or by the numbers you perish." Scriptural ministry in the church is so much larger than simply the number of bodies that show up on a Sunday morning. It does include this, but this is not the sole criterion for judging how the work of the church is going.

When you let your center speak, you are able to continue doing what you simply have got to do. You can do nothing else. You can do nothing less. You may not win a medal of honor, but by being true to yourself, you always can wear the badge of honoring what is deep within your soul.

EXCURSUS

> Matthew Kelly: Anyone who offers you an easy path is to be mistrusted. Life is difficult and messy; there is no point trying to mask that or pretend otherwise. But every situation you encounter is in need of one thing: a holy moment....Allow God to raise up the saint in you. This is what your corner of the world needs right now.[76]

---

76 Matthew Kelly, *Rediscover the Saints*, 12.

It would be nice if I could tell you that life really is a bowl of cherries and if you just do certain things and have certain attitudes you will be spared the pits that also come with cherries. Canned cherries come with the pits removed but they don't taste anything like the fresh cherries which come with pits in the middle. This is not a pessimistic view of life, it is simply another section in the frequently needed refresher course, Reality 101. In this kind of a world, Matthew Kelly maintains that what is needed are holy moments and we can provide them by allowing God to raise up the saint in each of us.

When Paul writes to the church at Corinth, he addresses them in a way that too many translations miss. In I Corinthians 1:2 he writes: *To the church of God that is in Corinth, to those who are sanctified in Christ Jesus, called Saints...* Contrary to the KJV, there is no "called *to be*" in the Greek text; they are "*called Saints*" (present tense). In Romans 15:25, Paul makes it clear that the designation "saints" applies to all Christians: *I am going to Jerusalem in a ministry to the saints."* The saint is already in us — we just need to allow God to raise it up and permit him to use us to create holy moments. What do holy moments look life? Well, here is one:

> Once, at a state dinner, a guest of Eleanor Roosevelt mistook the finger bowl for a beverage, picked it up with his hands, and began to drink. Without blinking, Mrs. Roosevelt picked hers up and drank as well, a gesture Flore believed represented the essence of good manners. "It's not about doing everything right," she explained. "It's about basic human decency, putting other people ahead of yourself."[77]

Holy moments are those moments made sacred by the gracious actions toward others that stem from our concern for them and not for ourselves. It has very little to do with "How will this look?" Putting other people at ease, helping another "save face," getting people off the defensive, giving a compassionate instead of a judgmental word or simply exhibiting basic human decency

---

77 Rachel Held Evans, *A Year of Biblical Womanhood*, 13.

are all ways to create holy moments. These are the ways to create moments of wonder.

> ...she said nothing, just smiled, looked into my eyes, and drew out a smile from within my soul.[78]

Sometimes making a difference in your world is as simple as this. There is an old song, "Little Things Mean a Lot," that provides a needed reminder. As one gets older, little things mean even more. Just the very presence of another person can make that difference. Thomas Keating tells of a Trappist monk who called asking if he might stop by for a visit. Keating gave an immediate, "Yes", and explains why: "His presence felt like a deep anchor into the unknown."[79] I cannot imagine the amount of prayer, meditation, reflection, and focus it must take to bring that kind of presence into a room. Wouldn't you like to meet the two people whose stories we have just told? Wouldn't it be a wonder?

SUMMATION

> One of the mottos of the Green Berets is: "Improvise, adapt, overcome." A lot of us were told as children, "If at first you don't succeed, try again." Sound advice, but as they say, "try again, then try something different."[80]

Making a difference in our world usually means more than having a hobby horse that we keep riding. "This is just who I am" tells me that someone has decided they don't need to do much improvising, adapting, or overcoming. They certainly don't feel they need to be different. Without stretching it too far, making a difference and being effective in an ever-changing world is always going to call for the need to improvise, adapt, overcome, and try something different. We're not talking about anything that is un-

---

78 Robert J. Wicks, *Riding the Dragon*, 52.
79 Elaine Pagels, *Why Religion?* (New York: HarperCollins, 2018), 129.
80 Angela Duckworth, *Grit* (New York: Scribner, 2016), 70.

true to that which speaks to us out of the center of our beings or stands opposed to that which we are certain is our calling.

These strategies of improvising, adapting, and overcoming are called for because life is not static and neither are we. Opportunities do not remain the same, our abilities do not stay on the same level, and circumstances frequently alter dramatically, calling for entirely new approaches and emphases. To keep playing in the same key when a new piece of music is handed to you would be unthinkable. Yet some people believe that we can pretty much do things as we have always done them and maintain our same level of harmony and effectiveness. Many have said that the famous last words of the church are: "Come weal or come woe, our status is quo." The status quo will not be the tool that keeps us making a difference in a world that refuses to remain settled down for very long.

One last word for those of us who are in the older category: What is the ideal age to retire? Never.[81]

As long as we live, I believe God intends for us to make a difference in our world, regardless of where that world is or however limited it appears to be. Huston Smith writes about his being in a nursing home and finally deciding that his role was to choose one person each day and discover some way to improve that person's life. In a small way? Probably. But in a nursing home those are the ways that count. It seems most appropriate that this account comes from a book titled *Tales of Wonder*.[82]

We don't retire because the world of wonder is not confined to any time or to any age. Disappointment and losses do not close out the chapter on possibilities. From his retirement home and his "secret diary," Henrik Groen gives this bit of wisdom:

> Without Edie and without the diary (this is his final entry), I will have time on my hands. Maybe I'll have to write a novel….I'll have to come up with another plan. As long as

---

81 Daniel J. Devitin, *Successful Aging* (New York: Penguin Random House, 2020), 378.
82 Huston Smith, *Tales of Wonder* (New York: HarperOne, 2009), 180.

there are plans, there's life. This afternoon I will go out and buy a new diary.[83]

QUESTIONS FOR REFLECTION AND CONVERSATION

1. Have you thought of small ways in which you could make a difference in your world?
2. What struck you most about the story of Desmond Doss?
3. Do you agree with the suggested age of retirement as "Never"?

---

83 Henrik Groen, *The Secret Diary of Henrik Groen*, 378.

9
REFUSE TO LIVE ON AUTOMATIC

SETTING THE STAGE

> Frederick Buechner: Literature, painting, music - the most basic lesson that all art teaches us is to stop, look, and listen to life on this planet, including our own lives, as a vastly richer, deeper, more mysterious business than most of the time it ever occurs to us to suspect as we bumble along from day to day on automatic pilot.[84]

Even if the crossing had a signal and a gate, the sign gave the first rule for safety: "Stop! Look! Listen!" As a boy, our group often took shortcuts, which meant crossing a railroad track several times before reaching our destination. Some had no signals or gates and the only warning would be the horn sounding from the locomotive. Stop, look, and listen could mean the difference between life and death.

Buechner suggests these three actions may indeed save us from missing out on a deeper and richer life. Living on automatic keeps us moving along without much real perception of what we are experiencing. Automatic pilot doesn't call for pausing in our hurried rush to somewhere else, turning up our hearing volume

---
84 Frederick Buechner, *Listening to Your Life,* 522.

and focusing on whatever is in our range of vision. We are talking about the difference between being alive instead of just plodding from one place to another.

Homer Martin and Christine Adams have written *Living on Automatic* which is one of my highly recommended books. On the back cover, one of the reviewers comments: "A must-read for anyone seeking new ideas and findings about their relationships." I would only add: "A must-read for anyone seeking ideas and findings about themselves." It contains revealing information on what makes us tick. Here is a paragraph from the last chapter, "How To Decrease Living on Automatic":

> When you are interacting, attempt to introduce your *thinking skills* rather than just reacting or responding based on your emotions and what you feel. Learn to *slow down* your automatic responses. When you sense a purely automatic emotional reaction, say, "Let me think about what you are saying or asking. I'll let you know my thoughts about this later."[85]

In that final chapter, the authors give "Five steps to free yourself from living on automatic." (They are fully unpacked in the book). Here is the opening line of each:[86]

1. Observe and think about *when and under what circumstances* your emotional responses take place.
2. Observe and think about *what will bring out* the emotionally conditioned behaviors, thoughts, and emotions in you and the other person.
3. Think about your *method of stopping your emotionally conditioned reactions,* be it your behaviors, thoughts, or emotions.
4. You need a way *to remind yourself to think* about your present situation instead of reacting with your conditioned emotional response.

---

85   Homer B. Martin and Christine B. L. Adams, *Living on Automatic* (Santa Barbara: Praeger, 2018), 166.
86   Ibid, 170-171.

5. *Take action* to communicate or reveal your decision after you have thought about the situation, gathered information, and decided on a path for yourself.

We will be touching on these principles as we move through this chapter. I can only imagine how many problem situations I could have avoided and how much richer my relationships would have been if I had possessed (and followed) these five steps.

REFLECTIONS

Not to review and learn from life is foolish. Moreover, if we don't constantly spend time asking ourselves about why we feel, think, and believe what we do, we will ruin the chance to live a freer, more satisfying life.

> Real prophets ask us the important questions: What voices are guiding you in life? Who from early life or contemporary culture is pulling your strings?[87]

A significant amount of both my morning and evening prayer time is spent in reflection. The morning time usually reflects responses to some reading I have done. One of my current morning reads requires a lot of reflecting, not only on what is printed in the book, but on things I believe and the way I do things in my life. I hesitate to recommend it because it is one of those books that requires a seat belt while reading and, even then, may result in a few loose teeth from the shaking! Why am I reading it? Because it makes me think, it makes me re-examine, it makes me look at things in a new light. It makes me ask better and deeper questions about the Christian faith and life in the church.

If you have ever seen the original *Frankenstein* movie, you recall the unusual introduction to this 1931 classic. It truly was a shocking kind of "horror" movie, very tame by current standards, but something so different that the producers felt an introduction was necessary. A curtain opens, and one of the performers address-

---

87 Ibid, 48, 56.

es the audience warning of some aspects of the movie that may prove rather shocking. His final sentences (as I remember them) go something like this: "You may not want to subject yourself to this and prefer to leave now....If not...well, you've been warned!"

I now give you the title of the book from which I will probably extract several quotes before I'm through with this work: *Take This Bread* by Sara Miles. Subtitle: *The spiritual memoir of a twenty-first-century Christian.*[88] One pre-text page endorsement reads: "This book is a stunner. Beautifully and simply written, it is a wonderfully straightforward account of a life and a conversion that will leave many readers, as it left me, tingling with longing that such signs and wonders might emerge in and through our own stories." It is definitely one of those recommended reads I mentioned in chapter 5 that bites and stings — and it definitely takes an axe to much of the solid ice of fixation, tradition, and boundaries.

I'll have to quickly add that often the Bible "upsets" me in the same way. Reading the Sermon on the Mount (Matthew 5 — 7), if done in full honesty, doesn't make one want to say "Amen!" but utter an exclamation, "Is Jesus serious?" Jesus knew it had a lot of shock value. Perhaps that is why he ended the "sermon" with a crash instead of an Amen! (We know he was serious because we are told he sat down before he began teaching. In the Synagogue, the rabbi stood to read the Scripture and was seated for the teaching.) Many seem to be in favor of posting the Ten Commandments but I've not heard any voices calling for the posting of the Sermon on the Mount which, if followed, would bring about drastic (and much needed) changes in individual lives and in the culture. Taken seriously, with all of its implications, it is a description of what it means to be born from above, to be born of the Spirit, to be a Kingdom citizen (John 3).

As mentioned earlier, a large part of my morning and evening prayer time is given to reflection. Reflecting on why I believe and feel about things the way I do is never quick, easy, or painless. It is necessarily an on-going process. Every day should provide a time

---

88   Sara Miles, *Take This Bread* (New York: Ballantine Books, 2007).

for questioning: Why do I believe what I believe? Why do I feel about certain situations (or people) the way I do? What are the things in my past that I am allowing to pull the strings in my present life? If I want to grow and develop more into the best version of myself, these are questions that cannot be ignored. Reflection is a process that must be used for this kind of analyzing, unless I intend to live on automatic.

I always end my day of reading with a piece of fiction, usually a mystery, more often than not, a British mystery. From one of these, set at Wimbledon, there comes this bit of wisdom on the part of the detective inspector solving her first case:

> As she went, the germ of an idea sprang to life in her mind. She thought about it as she continued walking. She decided to sleep on it and see if it survived the night.[89]

EXCURSUS

Changing our minds about what we believe or a perspective through which we view life, is not easy matter:

> Remember, too, that the narratives that keep you bound together are nearly impervious to direct attack.[90]
>
> One article suggested that the United States had found weapons of mass destruction in Iraq. The next article corrected the first. People on opposing sides of the political spectrum read the same articles and then the same corrections, and when new evidence was interpreted as threating to their beliefs, they doubled down. The corrections backfired.[91]
>
> Once something is added to your collection of beliefs, you protect it from harm. You do this instinctively and un-

---

89 Elizabeth Flynn, *Game, Set, Murder* (Oxford: Lion Fiction, 2013), 90.
90 David McRaney, *You Are Now Less Dumb* (New York: Gotham Books, 2013), 44.
91 Ibid, 144.

consciously when confronted with attitude-inconsistent information.[92]

Most scholars do not believe that Jesus' use of so many stories (parables) was accidental. It was his intentional strategy, not only to get the attention of his hearers, but to get them to do some serious thinking and feeling about the great issues of life and faith. He knew that the direct attack never worked, it only put people on the defensive. So, he used the indirect approach of the story. I cannot imagine a single parable that would not include as a part of the response on the part of the hearers, "We're going to have to think about that." When Jesus tells the parable of the sower (Luke 8:4f), about the ways we listen, how could you not ask yourself: "What kind of a listener have I been? Why do I provide no place for some seed ideas to grow? Why do I choke out others? What makes me give some ideas a large place to take root and influence my thinking and my feelings?"

In Luke 15, when Jesus tells the stories of a lost sheep, a lost coin, and a lost son, the hearers have a lot to carry home. "What does this tell me about my compassion for people in comparison to my compassion for a sheep? Could I be as forgiving as the Father? Would I be able to join the party for my brother or would I find myself outside the door?" When Jesus tells the parable of the tax collector and the Pharisee (Luke 18:9-14), the ones who "heard," would have to ask: "In which of those two do I see myself? Wonder why this is so?" On another occasion, Jesus tells the story about the vineyard's landowner who hires workers and at the end of the day pays the ones who had worked only an hour the same as those who had worked all day (Matthew 20:1-16). When the all-day workers complain about his unfairness, the owner asks: *"Are you envious because I am so generous?"* The astute hearers left that day asking themselves, "What does this tell me about God's grace and goodness? Am I glad to receive it in abundance but not quite so

---

92   Ibid, 145.

sure about the less deserving? Are there any but the less deserving to begin with?"

The crowd never left one of Jesus' teaching sessions with a simple set of rules. They left with much that needed to be processed, analyzed, and applied to life. There was always a need for re-thinking, re-examining, and the replacing of old ideas and emotions with some new ones.

A big sidebar is in order at this point: Beware of the halo effect that highjacks our thinking more often than we like to think:

> If we think a baseball pitcher is handsome and athletic, we are likely to rate him better at throwing the ball, too.[93]
>
> In the last one hundred years of research, beauty seems to be the one thing that most reliably produces the halo effect.[94]

The "halo effect" simply means that, because of one attractive feature, we assume a person is going to be good at other things that have nothing to do with that feature. Because most good mysteries are well-crafted stories about people and relationships, I'm not surprised at the insights to be gained from reading fiction. Here is a brief conversation from the previously cited British mystery:

"There's no need to panic. I don't think any of our suspects are going anywhere"

"Who have we got in the frame?" asked Derek.

"The front runners are Lavinia Bannister, Danny Moore, Philip Turnbull and Stewart Bickerstaff…What?" she asked as she saw Leanne's mouth turn down at the corners.

> "Oh, I wouldn't like to think it's Stewart. He's cute."[95]

The absurdity of the halo effect in this situation precipitates a lively discussion among the investigators of a crime. What does good looks have to do with whether or not a person should remain on the suspect list? Substitute any characteristic you particularly

---

93 Daniel Kahneman, *Thinking, Fast and Slow* (New York: Farrar, Straus, and Giroux, 2011), 199.
94 David McRaney, *You Are Now Less Dumb*, 89.
95 Elizabeth Flynn, *Game, Set, Murder*, 201.

favor and ask yourself if you are prone to judge people's suitability and gifts on the basis of something that is totally irrelevant. It's a good test to determine if our automatic pilot is engaged.

SUMMATION

Although it may not apply to every situation, I found a list of six basic steps to executing any change in life. I choose this for our summation because becoming aware of any automatic response on our part calls for change. If we intend to think and respond differently, we have to change. Here are Katherine Mansfield's six basic steps to executing any change in your life:[96]

1. AWARENESS: becoming conscious of the pattern or issue.
2. ACKNOWLEDGMENT — admitting that you need to release the pattern.
3. CHOICE — actively selecting to release the pattern.
4. STRATEGY - creating a realistic plan.
5. COMMITMENT — taking action, aided by external accountability.
6. CELEBRATION — rewarding yourself for succeeding.

QUESTIONS FOR REFLECTION AND CONVERSATION

1. How have you found yourself living on automatic?
2. How do you handle reflection? What about the author's suggestion of reading books and portions of Scripture that shake us up a little as one of the means for that reflection?
3. Have you ever noticed the "halo effect" in your evaluation of others?

---

96 Katherine Mansfield, *If Life is a Game.... These are the Rules* (Naperville, IL: Simple Truths, 1998), 61.

10
MAKE YOURSELF A HUMOR BEING

SETTING THE STAGE

> Within our personal chemistry we carry a medicine that reduces stress and prevents depression even more effectively than any pill. The energy/spirit/medicine I'm referring to is none other than your sense of humor or, as I choose to call it, your humor nature. To me humor nature is synonymous with human nature.[97]

I borrowed this chapter title from the title of the first chapter in Dr. Clifford Kuhn's book, *The Fun Factor,* published by Minerva Books, the publishing partner of the University of Louisville. Dr. Kuhn is popularly known as the "Laugh Doctor." He never suggests that people can laugh away all their troubles or medical problems. He never suggests that grieving is not a necessary part of dealing with loss. His emphasis in on not taking ourselves too seriously, being able to laugh at our foibles and attempts at perfection.

Dr. Kuhn gives 10 Fun Commandments. Here is number three: "Laugh at Yourself First":

---

97 Clifford Kuhn, *The Fun Factor* (Louisville: Minerva Books, 2012), 13.

This commandment is not about losing self-respect or demeaning ourselves. Just the opposite — it is an act of loving kindness. Willingness to laugh at ourselves frees us from the restrictions of the unrealistic and unremittingly harsh expectations to which we hold ourselves when we are under duress. It gives us latitude to appreciate the ever-present inconsistencies and contradictions that are part of our makeup.[98]

One of my favorite stories of how he uses humor is one he uses in both of his books. A very successful CEO comes to his office and complains that after achieving so many things, he feels trapped by his success and is not happy.

Tears welled up in his eyes. Embarrassed, he looked furtively around my office. "Where the hell are your tissues?" he grumbled. "You're a shrink, for God's sake. Surely you have a tissue."

"Do you want a new one or a used one?" I asked.

He looked at me sharply.

"The new ones cost extra," I said, keeping a straight face.

He looked confused. Then I saw a light of recognition in his eyes, and he burst into a laugh that lasted longer than my silly side joke warranted. When he caught his breath, he had a very different kind of tears in his eyes.

"That's the first good laugh I've had this week," he said. "I used to laugh all the time. That's what's missing!"[99]

Of course, it took more than a joke and one good laugh to unpack lots of things that helped this CEO redefine his life and redefine just what success is all about. But laughter definitely opened the door. Making himself a humor being enabled him to be a better human being. Here was a little bit of wonder brought about by the Laugh Doctor.

---

98 Ibid, 21.
99 Clifford Kuhn, *It All Starts With a Smile* (Louisville: Butler Books, 2007), 1-2.

REFLECTIONS

> An emotional appeal gets into your head better than a statistical analysis. A lecture sprinkled with jokes and unexpected turns will sway you more than one delivered via Power-Point slides.[100]

In all of my interims, I included a series of workshops that dealt with the things the congregation needed to do in order to be ready for the calling of a new pastor. In one of those sessions, I noticed that my wife was seated near the back of the room. One of the persons at the table was a woman who was not a very happy person, either in her personal life or in the church. After the session on our way home my wife told me about a discussion that followed one of my funny stories. "Is he always that silly?" enquired the very serious woman. "No," my wife responded. "Sometimes he's worse."

All my humor was relevant to the issue being discussed and none of it was "put-down" or "dark" humor. I believe it is much easier for people to hear and remember things that come with a little bit of humor rather than being delivered with the seriousness of mandates. Plus, this confession: humor comes easily for me and I enjoy using it because I have a good time with it as well as the congregation. In many of my sermons during the years I used the comic strip *Peanuts* because of the insights and wisdom that came wrapped in humor. One comment I read that affirmed my practice is this one: "In order to understand Jesus' teachings, we much have a sense of humor."[101]

Mary Poppins is not the only one who knows that "a little bit of sugar helps the medicine go down." If the issue you are presenting is serious and the opinions are quite divided, nothing helps like making your point with a humorous aside (not really so aside as it first seems). This calls to mind Barbara Bush and her commencement speech in 1990 at Wellesley College: "Who knows?

---

100 David McRaney, *You Are Now Less Dumb*, 45.
101 Kenneth S. Long, *The Zen Teachings of Jesus*, 20.

Somewhere out in this audience may even be someone who will one day follow in my footsteps and preside over the White House as the president's spouse — and I wish him well."[102] A direct attack on the issue she is addressing makes little difference. With this kind of humorous approach, who knows?

In 1985 Cal Samra wrote a book which I think calls for reissuing in today's tension-filled world: *The Joyful Christ: The Healing Power of Humor*.[103] Chapter one is titled: "Where Are All the Joyful Christians?" This is a good question in light of Jesus' promise: *"I have told you this so that my joy may be in you and your joy may be complete"* (John 15:11). One of the most fascinating parts of Samra's book is the collection of paintings showing Christ either smiling or laughing (I especially like "Jesus Laughing" by Willis Wheatley).[104] It seems more than obvious that crowds would not have flocked to this new rabbi, and children would not have been attracted to him, if he had been humorless. It has always amazed me how easily so many have missed the humor in Jesus' first great "sign" in John (the word this Gospel uses instead of miracle). It takes place at a wedding. After several days of celebration, when the host runs out of wine, Jesus turns some water into wine. *Now standing there were six stone water jars for the Jewish rites of purification, each holding twenty or thirty gallons* (John 2:6). Jesus produces between 120 and 180 gallons of the best wine that had been served. There must have been a lot of laughter at that wedding! (Couldn't resist!) Jesus must have loved a good wedding and a good party. (That is one of the charges brought against him by the Pharisees.) I can't keep from smiling when I read what happens afterward in John 2:11 b: *and his disciples believed in him.*

"Laughter is God's hand on the shoulder of a troubled world." Dr. McBride, a Phoenix psychotherapist, then comments on his thesis: "The cut-and-dried scientific approach to human life is

---

102 *Parade Magazine,* May 17-20, 2020.
103 Cal Samra, *The Joyful Christ: The Healing Power of Humor* (San Francisco: Harper & Row, 1985).
104 Ibid, 172-174.

one of the major catastrophes of today. The first symptom of the emotionally ill person is his lack of laughter."[105] An illustration of such a person is Friedrich Nietzsche, who was "a melancholy and dyspeptic man with a colossal ego. Nietzsche is regarded as the spiritual father of many of the humorless tyrants, including Hitler, who have terrorized the twentieth century with war and bloodshed."[106] The tragic irony of Nietzsche's life is that he spent his last years in a lunatic asylum, in the care of a group of gentle nuns.

The first time the word "laugh" appears in the Bible is in Genesis 17:17 following God's promise of a son to Sarah and Abraham: *Then Abraham fell on his face and laughed, and said to himself, "Can a child be born to a man who is a hundred years old? Can Sarah, who is ninety years old, bear a child?"* Later, when Sarah hears of the promise, she laughs (Genesis 18:12). The child born to them is named Isaac, which in the verb form means "God laughs" or "he laughs." Many have commented: First Abraham laughs, then Sarah laughs, and finally, God laughs with them.

EXCURSUS

I have always wanted to be Greek Orthodox on the Monday after Easter. It's their ancient custom to observe that day (Pascha) as a day of laughter — to celebrate the joke God played on Satan by raising Jesus. Jokes are the agenda for the day. I can't think of a better way to celebrate Easter than with peals of laughter.

My Seminary education did not include the name of Philip Neri. He was a sixteenth-century Catholic clown-priest who must have been a crowd-pleaser in Rome. Most contend he had two books he valued above all others: The New Testament and a book of jokes. "Like many clowns, he had both the gift of tears and the gift of laughter."[107] It has been my deep conviction, that when a congregation is able to weep together and to laugh together, they become a community. Even the Teacher of Ecclesiastes points out

---

105 Ibid, 22.
106 Ibid, 34.
107 Ibid, 107.

in all his dark pessimism that there is *a time to weep, and a time to laugh* (3:4). There is always time to reach down and touch those emotions that bring us more to ourselves and certainly closer to each other.

Norman Cousins is well-known for *The Anatomy of an Illness* in which he discusses the therapeutic value of humor. He maintains that twenty minutes of laughter (usually from classic comedies like Laurel and Hardy) gave him two hours of pain-free sleep. The good thing about prescribing laughter is that there are no negative side-effects. If you want to ruin your entire day, read all the possible side effects that can come from the medications you are taking. If you are taking multiple medications (as most of us oldies are doing), the assembled lists appear to greatly increase the odds of coming down with something far worse than the reason for taking the medications. After such a reading, my question was, "Where is Erma Bombeck when you need her?"

"At the height of laughter, the universe is flung into a kaleidoscope of new possibilities" (Jean Houston).[108] I have been in meetings where the injection of appropriate and relevant humor changed the entire atmosphere. It was like another group of people had replaced the group that had just been there. Laughter literally transformed the atmosphere and those who were seated in the room. Many a meeting was salvaged because laughter created a kaleidoscope of new possibilities.

SUMMATION

> Katherine Mansfield: "It is immense importance to learn to laugh at ourselves." When you learn to laugh at your mishaps you are able to instantaneously transform bad situations into opportunities to learn something about the absurdity of human behavior, most especially your own![109]

---

108 Clifford Kuhn, *It All Starts With a Smile*, 79.
109 Cherie Carter-Scott, *If Life is a Game....These are the Rules*, 56.

These words of advice seem especially necessary for those of us who are in any of what is termed the "helping professions." For those of us in pastoral ministry, it has never been summed up better than this: "The good news is you are a beloved child of God: the bad news is you don't get to choose your siblings."[110] The corollary is that not every member of the congregation got their choice in the selection of a pastor! The above quote cuts both ways. It didn't take me long to learn that I was not everyone's cup of ministerial tea. There are always different reasons for this. One person complained to another member that he had never had a pastor who got his sermons from the comic pages of the newspapers. I thought everyone would love my illustrations from *Peanuts,* but it was not to be. The best response to these kinds of complaints is to realize we simply cannot take ourselves too seriously and cannot take everything personally; there are always reasons someone has problems with another person that do not directly relate to that particular individual in any way. The worst thing to do is to "go serious."

One year, my wife gave me a DVD collection of Victor Borge broadcasts. If you are not familiar with this now departed gifted pianist, you missed one of the brightest comic geniuses of the last century. In each performance, he finally gets around to some masterful piano playing, but his mis-adventures and mis-steps are hilarious beyond words. In one episode, Borge was about ten minutes into his routine when a late-comer made his way into the second row. Borge stopped the show and asked the man, "Where are you from?" The response indicated a suburb of the city in which the theatre was located. Borge quipped, "That's interesting. I'm from Denmark and I got here before you did." That line was a show-stopper and the cleverest way I've ever heard of speaking to those whose disruptive late arrival is always an irritant to everyone. And, to show my age, Borge's was all good clean, creative humor with not an "F" word in sight.

Good humor enables me to see myself in others and that means it doesn't hurt quite so much. (Remember: ministers usually want

---

110 Rachel Held Evans, *Searching for Sunday,* 15.

to be people pleasers.) *The Secret Diary of Henrik Groen* spoke to me on many levels, especially since my ministry included many visits to retirement and nursing homes. His diary is loaded with hilarious and devil-may-care episodes, most of which he says are true, that illustrate just how important it is to be a humor being, especially as we get older. He writes that if his diary is ever published, he has come up with some possible titles:[111]

1. Down the Drain.
2. The Living End.
3. Over and Out.
4. The Last Hurrah.
5. Smoke Signals in a Hurricane (Sounds good but doesn't really apply here).

Knowing all the wonders that can come from laughter, I might want to title any diary I would publish: *Remaining a Humor Being All the Way Through Life*. After all, isn't that a good goal for all of us?

QUESTIONS FOR REFLECTION AND CONVERSATION

1. What did you think of Dr. Kuhn's strategy with the depressed CEO?
2. Have you ever experienced a time when humor drastically altered for the better some situation?
3. What do you think it means to be a humor being?

---

111 Henrik Groen, *The Secret Diary of Henrik Groen*, 359.

COMMIT TO DOWNWARD MOBILITY

SETTING THE STAGE

When Jesus washed the disciples' feet, he was showing them what leadership in the upside-down Kingdom of God looks like.[112]

…the God of Scripture stoops and stoops and stoops. At the heart of the gospel message is the story of a God who stoops to the point of death on a cross. Dignified or not, believable or not, ours is a God perpetually on bended knee, doing everything it takes to convince stubborn and petulant children that they are seen and loved.[113]

The first time Jesus tells his disciples about his forthcoming death and resurrection, Peter takes him aside and rebukes him (Mark 8:32). The next announcement brings this response: *But they did not understand what he was saying and were afraid to ask him* (Mark 9:32). When they reach their destination in Capernaum, Jesus asks them what they had been arguing about during the journey. *But they were silent, for on the way they had argued*

---

112 Rachel Held Evans, *Searching for Sunday*, 115.
113 Rachel Held Evans, *Inspired* (New York: Nelson Books, 2018), 12.

with one another who was the greatest (Mark 9:34). He takes their discussion seriously, which is reflected in his being seated (official teaching position of a rabbi), and calling his disciples to gather around. Then he says: *"Whoever wants to be first must be last of all and servant of all"* (Mark 9:35).

Kenneth Long explains one of the reasons most people do not take this seriously: "Paradoxes tend to be ignored in our society because we live in a world where rationality is king."[114] Even the disciples knew this was not the way things worked in their day. People fought to be first so they could be first. The last were always at the end of the line. It is just as difficult for us as it was for them to grasp the truth of this paradox of Jesus' Kingdom.

Luke appears to set the scene of the disciples' argument just before they enter the Upper Room (Luke 22:24). Ordinarily, the host would designate a servant to perform the menial task of removing the guest's sandals and washing the dust off their feet. "Since the meeting was obviously intended to be secret, no servants were present. None of the disciples was ready to volunteer for such a task, for each would have considered it an admission of inferiority to all the others."[115] It was only when Jesus took a towel and basin, knelt before each one of them, and washed their feet that they began to understand something of what he was talking about. Only John (chapter 13) records this episode along with Jesus' question: *Do you know what I have done to you?"* (John 13:12).

When the Son of God knells before each of his disciples and washes their feet, he turns the role of a servant into a divine ministry. He hallows the ground of service at the feet of another and turns the basin and the towel into badges of honor. He turns the task for which no disciple would volunteer, into a contest at their next meal to see who would be first to get the now sacred instruments of discipleship. He turns the space at the feet of each disciple into holy ground.

---

114 Kenneth S. Long, *The Zen Teachings of Jesus*, 61.
115 Frank E. Gaebelein, ed., *The Expositor's Bible Commentary*, Volume 9 (Grand Rapids: Zondervan, 1981), 136.

The kicker:

The transforming power of what happened in that Upper Room was not simply *what* Jesus did, it was *how* he did it. If he had grabbed the basin and towel with a disgusted look on his face that spoke his thoughts: "All of you think you're too good for this servant's job but while you sit there and protect your dignity, I'll shame you by doing the job myself." That kind of deed would have lacked any transforming power. Paul will later comment (I Corinthians 13) that deeds performed in this spirit are of no value whatsoever.

His parting "new commandment" had been simply stated: *"I want you to love each other as I have loved you"* (John 13:34). That night, each disciple experienced the touch of Jesus' love, exactly as they were — self-centered and caught up in their own self-importance. Jesus predicted that when his trial and the cross made their ugly appearances, they would run for cover. Holy Saturday would find them safely locked away from the Roman authorities. Sunday morning would not find them traveling with the brave women who go to anoint Jesus' body.

REFLECTIONS

> We may think we'd like to taste the life of celebrity, but those who have it, although they enjoy its perks, also feel its drawbacks and dangers — the obvious ones like lack of privacy and public criticism, and the less obvious such as disappointment that being a celebrity doesn't solve the riddle of life.[116]

The problem with ascertaining who is the greatest, found Jesus' disciples reflecting a basic human concern: status. It's all about how we stack up with others and a feeling that we somehow need to make it to the top of the stack, or at least somewhere near the top. That enables us to be in a position to look down on those who are below us. This also reflects an earlier scene when James

---

116 Thomas Moore, *Original Self* (New York: HarperCollins, 2000), 70.

and John request places of honor (one on his right and the other on his left) when Jesus sets up his Kingdom (Mark 10:35-41). When the other disciples learn of their request, we are told they are all bent out of shape (my translation). Probably because they hadn't thought to make the request earlier. I have always found it fascinating, that when Matthew gets ready to record the same incident, he does what the authors of Chronicles do in omitting embarrassing material about the kings, he paints a much better picture of the disciples and has the mother of James and John make the request (Matthew 20:20).

Once again, Jesus addresses the riddle of life that Thomas Moore is convinced is not solved by becoming a celebrity.

> *Jesus called them together and said, "You know that in this world kings are tyrants and officials lord it over the people beneath them. But among you it should be quite different. Whoever wants to be a leader among you must be your servant, and whoever wants to be first must be the slave of all. For even I, the Son of Man, came here not to be served but to serve others and to give my life as ransom for many"* (Mark 10:43-47, NLT).

Two quotations come to mind that speak to the same riddle of life — how do I become somebody? From several books and several sermons, I have heard the phrase "God wants you to be a winner!" Never once was the term "winner" taken out of the box so that we understood exactly what a winner looks like. These quotes speak to what Kingdom winners and losers look like:

> The more we move in the direction of placing ourselves at the center of things, the deeper we move into a life dominated by that which is contrary to and not in harmony with God and God's will.[117]

> *The Great Divorce* by C. S. Lewis: Hell is a state where everyone is perpetually concerned with his own dignity and advancement, where everyone has a grievance, and where ev-

---

[117] Perry Bramlett, Rueben P. Job & Norman Shawchuck, *30 Meditations on the Writings of C. S. Lewis* (Nashville: Abingdon, 2020), 71.

eryone lives the deadly serious passion of envy, self-importance, and resentment.[118]

Many true celebrities in God's Kingdom can easily go unrecognized. Most of the time what they do doesn't make a big enough splash to be picked up by the media (although not always the case). The "unsung heroes" go about their callings convinced that their "exceeding great reward" is simply in doing what they are called to do. Desmond Doss and his heroic rescue of seventy-five wounded men from the top of Hacksaw Ridge was mentioned earlier. In an interview that accompanies the movie on the DVD, a reporter asks him how it feels to be a hero. His reply is that he doesn't feel like a hero, he was just doing his job as a medic. But his heroic, "Lord, just one more," as voiced in the movie, has always touched me on a deep emotional level. There was never any, "Well, I've done enough and now it's time to get off this ridge." He never allowed himself to get into the center of things. It was never about him. That's the mark of a real winner.

EXCURSUS

> I myself do not really trust any spiritual teacher who is not up front and utterly honest about a necessary path of descending.[119]

Most often referred to as "Downward Mobility," this denotes an attitude of abandoning the effort to keep climbing as the major goal of life. Rachel Evans tells about a friend of hers, Kathy Escobar, who spent many years "climbing the leadership ladder at a megachurch in Denver before trading a life of religious success for what she calls a life of downward mobility inspired by the humility and poverty of Christ."[120] The confession and the process are worth noting:

---
118 Ibid, 114.
119 Richard Rohr, *The Universal Christ*, 218.
120 Rachel Held Evans, *Searching for Sunday*, 71.

Kathy, who describes herself as a recovering perfectionist and control freak, doesn't glamorize the process. She admits the healing happens at a slow pace and that this much diversity often leads to awkwardness and drama.... She says she'll never go back to the upward mobility life again.[121]

Before we pursue this idea further, some clarification is in order:

> To choose as Mother Teresa did, to live in the slums of Calcutta, amidst all the dirt and disease and misery, signified a spirit so indomitable, a faith so intractable, a love so abounding, that I felt abashed. — Malcolm Muggeridge.[122]

Mother Teresa had a unique calling that is not my calling. Sara Miles (referred to earlier) has a unique calling that is not my calling. These callings do not so much abash me (astonish and disconcert me) as they challenge me to find a calling of my own life that enables me to do "something beautiful for God." In another book, I discuss the question of whether it is better to be a big frog in a small pond or a little frog in a big pond and confess that my situation is more like being a frog in a puddle. When we consider the enormity of existence and our brief time journeying on this planet, that is essentially what it boils down to. All I need to do is what I am convinced is my calling, with the limited skills I have, in the small space and time in which I live, to the best that my imperfections will permit. I'm not called to be a Mother Teresa or a Paul or a Moses. I am called to be the best of what I can be with the gifts that are mine.

St. Therese of Lisieux (1873-1897) gave us "The Little Way" which she defined as doing the smallest actions with great love in the everyday and the ordinary. (This reminds me of Brother Lawrence who washed pots and pans in the monastery for the glory of God — and was later designated the "The Kitchen Saint"!). When you are freed from perfection and the constant demands of

---

121 Ibid, 72.
122 Malcolm Muggeridge, *Something Beautiful for God*, 21.

upward mobility, then you can give yourself to the everyday and the ordinary with pleasure, delight, and true service.

Big Warning:

Seeking downward mobility has nothing do with refusing to do our best and achieving all we are able to do. It does not mean that we put ourselves down (that is not humility) or refuse to have goals, dreams, and aspirations. The disciples were chastised because they argued about which one of them was the greatest. They wanted to be able to have an elevated position from which to look down on the others. They wanted a position that would mark off certain things and certain people as definitely "beneath them."

In the Sermon on the Mount, Jesus cautions about giving alms, praying, and fasting in such a way that it becomes a show for others to see. All of these are to be done "in secret" and God is the one who will hand out the recognition. Proverbs 27:2 puts it this way: *Let another praise you, and not your own mouth — a stranger, and not your own lips.* My simple advice is: Don't toot your own horn (like the Pharisees literally did when they gave alms). When giving this advice, someone invariably asks, "But what if no one else toots it?" My answer is always the same: "Then you remain tootless!" That may be the true mark of Downward Mobility!

SUMMATION

> We must not drift away from the humble works, because these are the works nobody will do. They are never too small. We are so small we look at things in a small way. Even if we do a small thing for somebody, God, being almighty, sees everything as great. For there are many people who can do big things. But there are few people who will do the small things.
> — Mother Teresa.[123]

---

123 Mother Teresa, *The Joy in Loving,* 222.

There are two very encouraging truths to be taken from this quote. First, if you are into the small things, there is not much competition and there will always be plenty of options. In the Upper Room that night, there was not much of a fight for the towel. The disciples had spent all their time arguing about the big things, about the great things (which Jesus later points out are not so great after all). There are so many little and ordinary things to be done. We should begin by selecting those we are certain we will be able to do with great love. Hopefully, this will lead to the expansion of our list. When this is done, the second encouraging truth belongs to us which is indicated by the title of the devotional book from which the above quote comes: *The Joy in Loving*.

Sara Miles writes about going outside two hours before the food pantry at her church opened and seeing eighty people already lined up:

> "A tiny, paranoid white woman who always spoke in a whisper was gesturing me over, urgently. I leaned in, and she took my arm, motioning to the skyline, where dark clouds were gathering over the hills of the city. The woman cleared her throat, 'Do you ever have days,' she whispered, 'when you feel like blessings are just being showered down on you?' I did."[124]

QUESTIONS FOR REFLECTION AND DISCUSSION

1. What do you consider the most difficult aspect of downward mobility?
2. How would you interpret what it means to love each other the way Jesus loves us?
3. Have you considered some small ways in which you might do "something beautiful for God?"

---

124 Sara Miles, *Take This Bread*, 205.

12
Keep Using Your Kingdom Glasses

SETTING THE STAGE

> The Psalms…transform what I have called our "worldview"….A "worldview" in this sense is like a pair of spectacles: it is what you look *through*, not what you look at.[125]

> The Greek word for repentance is *metanoia*, which means not so much being sorry as "changing your heart"….Spiritual awakening comes when we develop a radically new perspective on life.[126]

We probably have heard it said of someone, "He sees the world through rose-colored glasses." That person is not unique. The glasses may not be rose-colored but we *all* view the world through spectacles that largely determine our perspective on life. Our glasses are especially complex because they are made up of many different aspects of our lives that have gone into the makeup of our particular lenses.

John's ministry theme is summarized this way by Matthew (3:2): *"Repent, for the kingdom of heaven has come near."* Jesus begins his ministry on the same note (Matthew 4:17): *"Repent, for the*

125 N. T. Wright, *The Case for the Psalms*, 6.
126 Kenneth S. Long, *The Zen Teachings of Jesus*, 82-82.

kingdom of heaven has come near." The radically new perspective on life, the new spirit of the Kingdom, demanded by that repentance is spelled out in what is commonly labeled *The Sermon on the Mount.* The Beatitudes begin that sermon by briefly outlining the blessings that are present, not future, gifts to those who are: poor in spirit (open to the Kingdom), mourning, meek (lowly), hungering and thirsting for righteousness (justice), merciful, pure in heart, peacemakers, persecuted for living by the Kingdom principles.

The rest of the sermon (chapters 5 through 7 of Matthew) spells out what Kingdom citizens look like. They:

1. Are salt and light because of the way they live.
2. Fulfill the requirements of God's commandments better than the Pharisees do (lot of unpacking needs to be done here!).
3. Keep a check on anger.
4. Refuse to offer sacrifices in the Temple until things are made right with a person who has something against them.
5. Keep check on those attitudes, urges, and emotions within before they break out into wrongful acts.
6. Take very seriously the commitment required in marriage (another one that would take a book to discuss).
7. Live with such open honesty and integrity that nothing more is needed than a simple yes or no for the truth to be fully spoken.
8. Are not into retaliation in any form.
9. Know how to love even enemies by only wishing and doing good for them. (Jesus is "Kingdom serious" when he says this).
10. Never parades personal piety before others simply to be seen. Examples: offerings are silent experiences, not trumpet experiences; prays in secret and in simplicity - always privately to God alone; and, when fasting, does nothing to make it appear it is being practiced.
11. Are concerned about making eternal investments.
12. Make certain the light by which they live is healthy and whole.

13. Make certain God's will and purposes come before anything else in their lives.
14. Instead of worrying about the many insecurities of life, attempt to make trust in God's care and provisions the number one priority.
15. Refuse to be a judgmental person.
16. Exercise care in sharing their faith: Matthew 7:6 (another big unpacking job is needed here!).
17. Keep on asking, seeking, and knocking, knowing that such persistence leads to receiving, finding, and the opening of that which had been closed.
18. Make the Golden Rule their measuring stick for all relationships.
19. Check out the validity of the messages people tell them are from God by the lives these persons are living.
20. Recognize that talking a great faith is not the same as living a great faith.
21. Build their lives on the rock by not only hearing the words of Jesus but by living in obedience to them.

In plain English, this is a mouthful of demanding religion in anybody's book! It can easily be termed radical by today's standards and we haven't even finished with Jesus' teaching material in the remainder of Matthew's Gospel. This definitely calls for the wearing of Kingdom glasses.

REFLECTIONS

> It requires real changes in the physiology of your brain to accept new information demanding that you see the world in a new way.[127]
>
> One article suggested that the United States had found weapons of mass destruction in Iraq. The next article corrected the first....People on opposing sides of the political spectrum read the same articles and then the same corrections, and when

---
127 David McRaney, *You Are Now Less Dumb*, 154.

new evidence was interpreted as threatening to their beliefs, they doubled down. The corrections backfired.[128]

Once something is added to your collection of beliefs, you protect it from harm. You do this instinctively and unconsciously when confronted with attitude-inconsistent information.[129]

I remember the audiologist telling me an important fact about my new, first-time, hearing aids: "It will take two or three months for your brain to make the adjustments to this new method of hearing." She was right. Wearing Kingdom glasses is not a cure-all without recognizing that brain-adjustment is necessary. You have to train yourself to interpret what you are seeing (and hearing) in a new way. And it takes much longer than two or three months! Actually, it is the work of a lifetime.

Paul has some relevant advice: *Let the same mind be in you that was in Christ Jesus* (Philippians 2:5). Paul then gives what many believe is one of the first Christian hymns about Christ giving up his glory status to take the form of a human being who lived in total obedience to God — the obedience that led to the cross. In Philippians 4:8-9 Paul tells us what things we need to think about in order to begin to have the mind of Christ: *whatever is true, whatever is honorable, whatever is just, whatsoever is pure, whatever is pleasing, whatever is commendable,*.

The Bible is filled with admonitions about the "heart," which was believed to be the seat of both reason and emotion: *Above all else, guard your heart, for it affects everything you do* (Proverbs 4:23, NLT). Putting on Kingdom glasses is step number one, guarding our minds; filling them with all that makes for wholeness is step number two. We touched on this in the chapter on reading and I don't want to begin another tirade against Facebook and other social media outlets that permit any information whatsoever to be sent out without any validation. I don't see any checks and balances

---

128 Ibid, 144.
129 Ibid, 145.

Wonder Where the Wonder Went

in the near future so it is up to each of us to fill our minds with things that are honest, true, and of good report.

Everyone now seems to have a platform for whatever pops into their heads. Applicable only for its comic relief is this classic line from Christopher Hitchens: "Everybody has a book in them, but in most cases that's where it should stay."[130] The larger application all too quickly comes to mind.

Since brain transplants are not feasible, the information we give our brains must be carefully evaluated. Too many have already observed: "There is certainly an information explosion today. The tragedy is that we not having a similar wisdom explosion."

EXCURSUS

> I also thought, "As long as I am down here in the spiritual basement, I might as well look around." And I did....I realized I had forgotten about faithfulness and replaced it with a shallow desire for success.[131]

Putting on Kingdom glasses ought to enable us to see the number one requirement for all its citizens. The good news is that the requirement can be met by anyone regardless of educational level or status assigned by the world. It is a requirement that does not demand more than we are able to give. It is requirement that is suited to everyone whoever, wherever, and however we are. It is a requirement that makes possible for all to hear the commendation, "Well done." The basic requirement for Kingdom citizens is: faithfulness.

That involves: Faithfulness to the calling you believe belongs to you, faithfulness based on the best you can do with the gifts you have. Faithfulness that is not based on comparison with anyone else who might happen to have a similar calling. Faithfulness that has the basic rule of thumb: "All things considered." My wife laughingly says she wants her epitaph to read: "All things con-

---
130 Lee Eisenberg, *The Point Is,* 157.
131 Robert J. Wicks, *Riding the Dragon,* 11.

sidered, she did pretty well." Gratefully, the One who is going to make the final evaluation of our lives is the One who fully knows and understands all the things that need to be considered.

When Rachel Evans talks about the twenty-three volunteers who work weekly in the church's food pantry, she notes that all except two of them come from the lines of people waiting for the pantry to open. One person sums-up what she sees in the group of volunteers:

> Martha still referred to the volunteers as misfits, from "the island of misfit toys." We had several ex-junkies, a number of folks living on disability because of mental illness, four guys with varying attention and temper problems who all belonged to the same head-injury support group. And yet these were the people who were solving the problems of the pantry — and also showing me the dimensions to the work that I couldn't have imagined when I first started seeing the pictures of groceries around the Table.[132]

You have to wonder if God saw them as misfits from the island of misfit toys or if he saw them, all things considered, as faithful stewards in a program of feeding the poor and the hungry. When I pondered this and looked over my sixty years of ministry and all the volunteers who worked in various programs and ministries of the church, I wonder how God saw us (I include myself). At times it must have looked like we, too, had come from some island of misfits but, at the moment, we seemed to be fitting right in to the place God had called us. At least we all seemed to be faithful. We really need to strike out "at least" in the preceding sentence and rewrite: "Most importantly, we all were faithful to the tasks to which we had been called."

SUMMATION

I want to give a brief illustration of what it means to be wearing Kingdom glasses in this broken world. It comes from Rachel

---

132 Sara Miles, *Take This Bread*, 208.

Held Evans and her discussion of Philip and the Ethiopian Eunuch found in Acts 8:26-39. The eunuch was returning from worship in Jerusalem and was in his carriage reading aloud (the way everybody read in those days) from Isaiah 53:7-8. Philip explains what he was reading and how it applies to Jesus Christ. The eunuch then asks: *"Look! There's some water! Why can't I be baptized?"* (NLT). Here is what Rachel Evans says about this incident:

> (As a eunuch, this man would have been strictly prohibited from even entering the temple grounds, much less participating in its rituals: Leviticus 21:20; Deuteronomy 23:1.) "Philip baptized the eunuch in the first body of water the two could find….Philip got out of God's way. He remembered that what makes the gospel offensive isn't who it keeps out, but who it lets in. Nothing could prevent the eunuch from being baptized, for the mountains of obstruction had been plowed down, the rocky hills had been made smooth (Isaiah 53:7-8), and God had cleared a path. There was holy water everywhere. Two thousand years later, John's (the baptizer) call remains a wilderness call, a cry from the margins."[133]

With Kingdom glasses we see all ground as holy ground and all water as holy water. We can do God's holy work anywhere and can baptize with mercy and grace any who ask, "Why can't I be baptized?" The lines of the song I learned as a boy remain true: "Whosoever will to the Lord may come. He will not turn away."

I might not know that, I might not see that, if I were not wearing Kingdom glasses.

QUESTIONS FOR REFLECTION AND DISCUSSION

1. Have you ever considered what kind of glasses you are wearing that is determining how you see things?
2. How difficult have you found it to see things in a different way?

---

[133] Rachel Held Evans, *Searching for Sunday,* 39.

3. What do you think about the author's suggestion that faithfulness is what success looks like for the Kingdom citizen?

Epilogue:
Wonder in God's Broken World

N. T. Wright has written a paragraph that caused me to write "great perspective" in the margin.

> What you do in the Lord is not in vain. You are not oiling the wheels of a machine that's about to roll over a cliff. You are not restoring a great painting that's shortly going to be thrown on the fire. You are not planting roses in a garden that's about to be dug up for a building site. You are — strange though it may seem, almost as hard to believe as the resurrection itself — accomplishing something that will become in due course part of God's new world. Every act of love, gratitude, and kindness, every work of art or music inspired by the love of God and delight in the beauty of his creation, every minute spent teaching a severely handicapped child to read or to walk; every act of care and nurture, of comfort and support, for one's fellow human beings and for that matter one's fellow nonhuman creatures; and of course every prayer, all Spirit-led teaching, every deed that spreads the gospel, builds up the church, embraces and embodies holiness rather than corruption, and makes the name of Jesus honored in the world — all of this will find its way, through the resurrecting power of God, into the new creation that God will one day make.[134]

---

134 N. T. Wright, *Surprised by Hope: Rethinking Heaven, the Resurrection, And the Mission of the Church* (New York: HarperOne, 1961), 19.

This is an encouraging reminder that the greatest wonder of all remains our basic hope for the future. One writer posed the question: "Imagine yourself at 90 years old, looking back over your life. What do you want to see?"[135] I wrote in the margin of the book: "I want to keep looking forward!!!" At eighty-five, people like to remind me that I have a lot more past than I have future. I quickly tell them they are mistaken. I have so much more future that the past seems more like the blink of an eye.

Arthur Schopenhauer said: "To our amazement we suddenly exist, after having for countless millennia not existed; in a short while we will again not exist, also for countless millennia. That cannot be right says the heart."[136] Something within us simply bears witness to being created for more than a few short years on planet earth. Scripture tells us we are children of God and thereby children of eternity. N. T. Wright echoes the Scripture: our labor is not in vain. All that we do will certainly find its way into the new creation God will one day make.

One of my current nightly devotional reads is Mother Teresa's *The Joy in Loving*. This reading seemed especially relevant:

> Often, we see small and big wires, new and old, cheap and expensive electric cables that are useless, for until the current passes through them there will be no light. The wires are you and me, the current is God. We have the power to let the current pass through us — to use us — or refuse to be used and allow the darkness to spread.[137]

God has chosen to use us as some of his wonders in this world. What a blessing and a wonder this is for each of us. We have the opportunity to be the wonder we are looking for.

Amen and amen!

---

135 Cherie Carter-Scott, *If Life is a Game....Here Are the Rules*, 125.
136 Lee Eisenberg, *The Point Is*, 22.
137 Mother Teresa, *The Joy in Loving*, 219.

Bibliography of Quoted Sources

Aslan, Reza. *Zealot.* New York: Random House, 2013.

Bramlett, Perry, Job, Rueben P. & Shawchuck, Norman. *30 Meditations on the Writings of C. S. Lewis.* Nashville: Abingdon, 2020.

Buechner, Frederick. *Listening to Your Life.* New York: HarperSanFrancisco, 1992.

Carter-Scott, Cherie. *If Life is a Game….Here are the Rules.* Naperville, IL: Simple Truths, 1998.

Christian Century. May 20, 2020.

Coles, Robert. *Harvard Diary II.* New York: Crossroad Publishing, 1997.

Cruden, Alexander. *Cruden's Complete Concordance to the Old and New Testaments.* Philadelphia: The John C. Winston Company, 1949.

Devitin, Daniel J. *Successful Aging.* New York: Penguin Random House, 2020.

Duckworth, Angela. *Grit.* New York: Scribner, 2016.

Eisenberg, Lee. *The Point Is.* New York: Twelve, 2016.

Evans, Rachel Held. *Inspired.* New York: Nelson Books, 2018.

_____.*Searching for Sunday.* Nashville: Nelson Books, 2015.

_____. *A Year of Biblical Womanhood.* Nashville: Nelson Books, 2012.

Flynn, Elizabeth. *Game, Set, Murder.* Oxford: Lion Fiction, 2013.

Frankl, Victor. E. *Man's Search for Meaning.* Boston: Beacon Press, 1959.

Gaebelein, Frank E., ed. *The Expositor's Bible Commentary.* Volume 9. Grand Rapids: Zondervan, 1981.

Goldstein, Niles Eliot. *God at the Edge.* New York: Bell Tower, 2000.

Groen, Henrik. *The Secret Diary of Henrik Groen.* New York: Grand Central Publishing, 2014.

Homiletics, Volume 10, Number 2. March-April, 1998.

Kahneman, Daniel. *Thinking, Fast and Slow.* New York: Farrar, Straus, and Giroux, 2011.

Kelly, Matthew. *Rediscover the Saints.* North Palm Beach: Blue Sparrow, 2019.

Kuhn, Clifford. *The Fun Factor.* Louisville: Minerva Books, 2012.

_____. *It All Starts With a Smile.* Louisville: Butler Books, 2007.

Long, Kenneth S. *The Zen Teachings of Jesus.* New York: Crossroad, 2001.

Malone, Nancy. *Walking a Literary Labyrinth.* New York: Riverhead Books, 2003.

Mansfield, Katherine. *If Life Is a Game...These are the Rules.* Naperville, IL: Simple Truths, 1998.

Marlette, Doug. *The Bridge.* New York: HarperCollins, 2001.

Martin, Homer B. and Adams, Christine B. L. *Living on Automatic.* Santa Barbara: Praeger, 2018.

McRaney, David. *You Are Now Less Dumb.* New York: Gotham Books, 2013.

Miles, Sara. *Take This Bread.* New York: Ballantine Books, 2007.

Miller, Calvin. *Life is Mostly Edges.* Nashville: Thomas Nelson, 2008.

Moore, Thomas. *Original Self.* New York: HarperCollins, 2000.

Muggeridge, Malcolm. *Something Beautiful for God.* San Francisco: Harper & Row, 1971.

Murphy, Kate. *You're Not Listening.* New York: Celadon Books, 2019.

New Jerusalem Bible. New York: Doubleday, 1985.

New King James Bible. Nashville: Thomas Nelson Publishers, 1982.

New Living Translation. New York: American Bible Society, 1996.

New Revised Standard Bible. Grand Rapids: Zondervan Publishing House, 1989.

Nouwen, Henri J. *Bread for the Journey.* New York: HarperOne, 1997.

_____. *The Mystery and the Passion.* Minneapolis: Fortress Press, 1992.

O'Day, Gail R. and Peterson, David L., eds. *Theological Bible Commentary.* Louisville: Westminster John Knox Press, 2009.

Pagels, Elaine. *Why Religion?* New York: HarperCollins, 2018.

Parade Magazine. May 17-24, 2020.

Peterson, Eugene. *The Message.* Colorado Springs: Navpress, 2002.

Phillips, J. B. *The New Testament in Modern English.* New York: The Macmillan Company, 1985.

Platt, Christian. *Post Christian.* New York: Jericho Books, 2014.

Poe, Harry Lee. *Christian Witness in a Postmodern World.* Nashville: Abingdon, 2000.

Revised English Bible. Oxford: Oxford University Press, 1989.

Rohr, Richard. *Immortal Diamond.* San Francisco: Jossey-Bass, 2013.

_____. *The Universal Christ.* New York: Convergent, 2019.

Samra, Cal. *The Joyful Christ: The Healing Power of Humor.* San Francisco: Harper & Row, 1985.

Smith, Huston. *Tales of Wonder.* New York: HarperOne, 2009.

Steff, Tom. *A Faith Worth Believing.* New York: HarperSanFrancisco, 2004.

Teresa, Mother. *The Joy in Loving.* New York: Viking, 1996.

Thompson, Frank Charles, ed. *The New Chain-Reference Bible.* Third Improved Edition. Indianapolis: B. B. Kirkbride Bible Co., 1934.

Tickle, Phyllis. *The Divine Hours: Prayers for Summertime.* New York: Doubleday, 2000.

Today's New International Version. Grand Rapids: Zondervan, 2005.

Wicks, Robert J. *Crossing the Desert.* Notre Dame: Sorin Books, 2007.

_____. *Riding the Dragon.* Notre Dame, Sorin Books, 2012.

Wright, N. T. *The Case for the Psalms.* New York: HarperOne, 2013.

_____. *Surprised by Hope: Rethinking Heaven, the Resurrection, and the Mission of the Church.* New York: HarperOne, 2008.

Wuest, Kenneth S. *The New Testament, An Expanded Translation.* Grand Rapids: William B. Eerdman's Publishing Company, 1961.

Paperback: $14.99
eBook: $7.99

https://www.energiondirect.com/product/finding-stability-in-uncertain-times/

www.ingramcontent.com/pod-product-compliance
Lightning Source LLC
LaVergne TN
LVHW041631070426
835507LV00008B/558